Introduction to
Music Education

Fourth Edition

Introduction to Music Education

Fourth Edition

CHARLES HOFFER
University of Florida

WAVELAND
PRESS, INC.
Long Grove, Illinois

For information about this book, contact:
Waveland Press, Inc.
4180 IL Route 83, Suite 101
Long Grove, IL 60047-9580
(847) 634-0081
info@waveland.com
www.waveland.com

10-digit ISBN 1-4786-3407-3
13-digit ISBN 978-1-4786-3407-2

Printed in the United States of America

7 6 5 4 3 2

To

Andrew Allan Hoffer

Kendall Renee Hoffer

Emily Claire Hoffer

Lauren Ruth Hoffer

Lucas Latham Teater

Kevin Robert Teater

May the joy of music fill their lives

Contents

Preface

So you are thinking about becoming a music teacher. Great choice! It's a job that is interesting, challenging, and meaningful. It is also a role that requires much understanding, both of the subject of music and how it can benefit people, especially school students.

Topics covered in this book explore the teaching/learning process, personal qualities of successful music teachers, and planning music instruction. Typical college programs for preparing music teachers are examined along with the music education profession.

An analysis of elementary and secondary school music programs is included, as well as challenges and opportunities that school music teachers face today. Future music educators are asked to think about their long-range career goals.

The fourth edition is not a methods textbook. Such courses are the logical next step in most teacher education programs and are usually taken in the junior and senior years.

I would like to thank the many colleagues who have over the years provided me with ideas and guidance in my teaching and writing about music education. Citing a few names would not be fair to the many who are not mentioned. I can only recognize them here as a group.

Special thanks are due my wife, Mimi, for her many valuable suggestions and contributions to this edition.

The Importance of Teaching Music

1

It all begins here. It has to. Unless music is valuable for people, especially young people, then the whole idea of music education is in deep trouble. If music makes little or no difference in the lives of people, there is little point in spending time and effort educating them in it. For this reason, music education begins with a clear understanding of why it is important to people and the quality of their lives.

For present and future music teachers there is an additional reason why music education begins with the importance of teaching and learning music. Those reasons have a lot to do with what and how music should be taught. For example, if music is seen as a nice extra-curricular activity with little educational content, then music teachers don't need to be concerned about what students learn. On the other hand, if music is seen as something that's a vital part of a young person's education, then music teachers will take actions to ensure every student acquires basic music skills and knowledge. The reasons for music in schools not only provide a starting place, they also point to the direction for music education.

The photograph on the next page makes the point very effectively: life without music would be pretty bleak and dreary. People would not physically die if they didn't have music, but some of the quality of their lives would be missing. Psychologically they would be worse off, and their spirits would be diminished and dampened. Music contributes to the quality of people's lives.

The message on the photograph, "Imagine the world without music," also applies to societies and civilizations. Without music, the

IMAGINE
THE WORLD
WITHOUT
MUSIC

quality of life in America would be less than it is. It would lack some of its vitality and vigor. The nation would be poorer, not only economically, but also in how its citizens act and feel.

Music and the other arts represent an important difference between existing and living. Animals exist in the sense that they manage to survive. Humans live; they attempt to make life interesting and satisfying. Humans are not content just to get by, to survive. Music, the visual arts, and dance enrich life and bring to it special meanings by providing an avenue for expression. People admire the shifting surf, the colors of a sunset, and the beauty of a flower. They also create objects they can contemplate and with which they can enrich their lives. Although a large cardboard box could serve as a nightstand by a bed, most would rather have a wooden table or piece of furniture with some grace and beauty. The compulsion of humans to reach beyond their immediate and practical needs is not just a luxury; it is an essential quality of being human.

People sense the value of music, even if they seldom talk about it. One could assemble a large number of impressive statistics about the time and money people spend on music, the number of persons who attend concerts and buy recordings in one form or another, the number who play a musical instrument or sing in choirs, and so on. Music has been present in every society since the dawn of civilization. It is found in every part of the globe, from the remote areas of Africa and Australia to the streets of Chicago and Beijing.

The importance of music to people is demonstrated in so many ways that it's easy to overlook them. Just about every film and television show has a sound track, which almost always contains theme music. Music is included in public events such as pregame activities, celebrations of ship launchings, and the swearing-in ceremonies of public officials. People are exposed to music in supermarkets, airports, and their cars. People can hardly avoid music when they are away from their residence.

A fundamental point is clear: *music is important to people*. The point may be obvious, but it is essential. If music were not important to people, then the teaching and learning of it would be irrelevant.

THE EXPERIENCE OF TEACHING

For music teachers, the rationales and supporting data for music in the schools are reassuring, but logic and facts are not the primary reason for their choice of vocation. For them, teaching is a personal experience. It's a job that becomes meaningful and satisfying because of their experiences with young people.

They remember students like the boy who, in spite of his small size, was determined to play trombone. Although it was tough going for him at first, he learned to play it well, and he continued to do so throughout high school. They remember students like the nice boy who suffered from a palsied condition that left him with slurred speech and a tendency to become faint during performances of the high school choir. (Two husky boys were placed on each side of him to ease him down so he could sit on the risers if he began to feel weak.) They remember how they were saddened a few years later when they heard that he drowned while swimming. They wondered, "Did I do all I could have done for him when he was in choir?"

They remember others, too, including the eager fifth grade trumpet student who couldn't wait to try the valve oil the store placed in her case. She didn't wait for instructions before she began to dribble the oil on the outside of the valves and then on to her lap. They also remember the hundreds of youngsters who were introduced to the music of Handel, Bartók, and Sousa and found in those works a world of music they hardly knew existed before. These and countless other experiences convince music teachers of the value of their work. They know music is well worth studying; no one need tell them. Although, of course, they enjoy hearing appreciative comments from parents, school administrators, or other teachers.

They also are aware of what their students would miss if there were no music instruction in the schools. They know the students would be severely limited in their knowledge about music and their ability to be involved with it. The few students who possess unusual ability or come from families able and willing to pay for private instruction in music will be fine. However, most students would:

- have no experience in a vocal or instrumental ensemble;
- be unable to use music notation;
- have very limited skill in listening to music;
- know only a very small number of songs of only one or two types;
- seldom have a chance to try creating music;
- know little about important aspects of Western music and the different types of music around the world; and
- have much less favorable attitudes toward music.

In short, they would be deprived—cheated may be a better word for it—of knowing about music beyond a marginal level.

Because of their experiences in teaching and knowledge of what a good music program should be, most music teachers take their work seriously. As with any profession, there are a few members who fall short, but the great majority of music teachers in schools are able men and women who care about having their students learn. That's the way it should be, of course, but it can cause feelings of frustration and disappointment when school administrators or parents appear to regard music in a lackadaisical way. The conscientious music teacher may wonder: "Why don't they understand what the students are getting from their music classes?"

Music teaching is a personal matter for yet another reason. Often a music teacher is the only one in that area in the school, or at least the only one in a particular music specialty in the school. It's a rare high school that has two choral directors, for example. Professionally speaking, most music teachers feel isolated. They seldom have a chance to discuss their work with other music teachers. This fact increases the importance of NAfME (the National Association for Music Education) and its state-affiliated units.

It also means music teachers must be more self-directed and responsible than teachers of other subjects. They must be the developers, facilitators, and evaluators of their work. They must also be the communicators about their work to school administrators and parents to a degree not true of English or science teachers. For these reasons, teaching music is challenging, interesting, and very worthwhile.

THE NEED FOR INSTRUCTION

The fact that music is important does not automatically ensure music's place in the school curriculum. It is possible to understand the value of music in people's lives yet fail to think music should be taught in schools. For example, a person might think music can be learned casually in life, like learning to ride a bicycle. Such a view would be true if an education in music consisted only of learning to sing a few simple songs by rote. However, just as an education in mathematics consists of much more than learning how to add and subtract, and an education in science means more than observing the patterns in the weather, an education in music involves much more than a little singing or superficial listening. Young people need to be taught reading, science, math, and history, and they also need to be taught music.

The second major point is this: The learning of any subject, including music, beyond a rudimentary level requires organized, systematic instruction, usually from a trained professional. There is simply too much to be learned in today's world for areas of knowledge to be left to the random circumstances of family or social conditions. The schools may not always do things as well as they should, but they fulfill a function in society that most families cannot. A system of education is necessary in today's complex societies. And for most students, if they are going to be educated in music, it will happen in the schools—or it won't happen at all.

Fortunately, most people not only value music, but they also sense the value of young people learning music. Even if they can't express the reason why they think this is so, they feel it intuitively. When they hear a group of young people making music, even if it's not performed particularly well by trained musicians' standards, they know in their hearts it is a good thing. Perhaps it is because of the feelings encouraged in them when they hear a group of young people doing something constructive, or perhaps they sense that music contributes to the quality of life in the community and its young people. Whatever their reasons, most adults want young people to have a well-rounded education that includes music.

Again, it is possible to assemble impressive statistics about the number of schools offering music programs, the amount of money raised by support groups for music activities, positive responses to opinion polls, and so on. The problem with support for music is not the availability of at least some music instruction in schools but rather the establishment of programs of sufficient scope and quality. High-quality school music programs often cost more than some other areas of the curriculum, and there is a lot of competition for the limited funds available to education. In addition, music educators have usually not been diligent in educating school officials and the public about what a good school music program should be like. This important matter is discussed later in this book.

THE NATURE OF AESTHETIC EXPERIENCES

The word "music" covers a lot of territory. It runs from the tunes people whistle while washing a car, to pieces teenagers use to identify themselves with a particular group, to music created to inspire patriotic or religious feelings, to complex musical works that affect our psychological beings. There are many kinds of music for many different purposes, just as there are many different types of clothes, most of which are appropriate for only certain uses and occasions, like tuxedos and sweat suits.

Music, especially music for the concert or recital hall, can add a dimension to life that is available only through the arts. Whether one calls it "subjective reality," "aesthetic world," "world of feeling," "artistic," "poetic," or something else, it has to do with thinking and experiences that are richer and often have more effect on people than rational, cognitive thinking. Sometimes these aesthetic experiences are truer in terms of expressing how people feel. In any case, they are a valuable aspect of human life.

The following lines from the Old Testament (Isaiah 55:12) describe how the ancient Israelites will feel when they are freed from Babylon.

For you shall go out in joy,
and be led forth in peace;
the mountains and the hills before you
shall break forth into singing,
and all the trees of the field
shall clap their hands.

Taken literally, the lines don't make much sense. Everyone knows trees have no hands and mountains can't sing. But in getting across the message of how the Israelites will feel, the lines are far more expressive than merely saying, "You are going to feel mighty good when you are freed." Of course, everyday communication would be nearly impossible if only artistic, poetic discourse were used. But a life filled with only objective, rational thought would be drab and tedious.

Aesthetic experiences differ from ordinary experiences in a number of ways. One basic difference between aesthetic and ordinary experiences is the nonpractical nature of aesthetic experiences. They are valued for the insight, satisfaction, and enjoyment they provide, not for any practical benefits. Looking at a bowl of fruit (a scene frequently painted by artists) is aesthetic when you contemplate the color and shape of the pieces of fruit. It is not aesthetic when you are thinking about how the fruit reminds you that you are hungry. An aesthetic experience is an end in itself; it is done only for the value of doing it.

A second characteristic of an aesthetic experience is that it involves both intellect and emotion. When you look at a painting aesthetically, you are consciously aware of considering thoughtfully its shapes, lines, and colors. That's the intellectual part. At the same time you are reacting to what you see; you have feelings about the painting, even if it's abstract. Seldom are these reactions so strong that you start laughing or crying, but you react to some degree. Your feelings are involved.

Because intellectual contemplation is required, recreational activities like playing tennis, or purely physical sensations such as standing under a cold shower, are not considered aesthetic. Neither are purely intellectual efforts such as working multiplication problems, although even in such a case, a reaction is often involved, as when you see an error like $3 \times 8 = 25$.

A third characteristic of aesthetic experiences is that they are experiences. You cannot tell someone about a painting or a musical work and expect that person to derive the same amount of enjoyment from the work that you did. In fact, telling about a piece of music or a drama tends to ruin it. For this reason, aesthetic experiences have no answers, as do problems in a math class. Listening to the last minute of Beethoven's Fifth Symphony is not the "answer" to that symphony. Anyone who tries doing so is cheating themselves out of the aesthetic enjoyment that the symphony can provide.

A fourth characteristic of aesthetic experiences is focusing attention intently on the object being contemplated. This centering of attention is on the object itself as an object, not on a task to be accomplished such as making a good serve when playing tennis.

Where does the idea of beauty enter the discussion of aesthetic experiences? In one sense, it doesn't very much. Not all aesthetic experiences need to be beautiful in the usual sense of that word. Hundreds of works of art, from Stravinsky's *The Rite of Spring* to the Ashcan school of painting of Edward Hopper and George Bellows, have demonstrated that the aesthetic and the beautiful are two different considerations.

Pointing out what an aesthetic experience is not helps to clarify its nature. The opposite of aesthetic is not ugly or unpleasant, but rather it might be thought of as "anesthetic"—no feeling, no life, nothing. An example of anesthetic behavior that comes to mind happened one day while I was observing a mediocre middle school band rehearsal. A sousaphone player was chatting with one of the drummers when the band director started the rehearsal without waiting for the players who were not paying attention. After a few moments, the sousaphone player realized he should be playing along with the others. Although he didn't know where they were in the music or what to play, he pulled the mouthpiece to his mouth and started blatting away—with no sense of what was happening musically.

Nonmusical Reasons for Music

Music has a long tradition of being included in schools for reasons such as citizenship, character development, team spirit, and health benefits. Plato, in his *Republic*, cites the need for music in the education of every citizen. His reasons were based on the ancient Greek idea of ethos—the belief that each mode promoted certain qualities of character in a person. Because music was closely allied with mathematics during the Middle Ages, music was one of the main subjects in medieval universities, and scholars were fascinated with the acoustical ratios of musical sounds. They wondered if the ratios might reveal secrets about the universe. In 1837, when Lowell Mason was given permission to begin teaching music in the Boston schools, the subject was justified because it contributed to reading and speech and provided "a recreation, yet not a dissipation of the mind—a respite, yet not a relaxation—its office would thus be to restore the jaded energies, and send back the scholars with invigorated powers to other more laborious duties" (Birge, 1966, p. 43).

The belief that music has the power to help people in ways other than aesthetically did not end with Lowell Mason. In fact, until after the middle of the twentieth century, nonmusical reasons were almost the only ones offered for music in the schools. For example, in 1941, Peter Dykema and Karl Gehrkens, two major figures in the development of American music education, wrote that "the teacher teaches the children through the medium of music" (pp. 380–381). The implication of their view is that music should be in the schools to help achieve goals beyond itself. In 1991, the report of the National Commission on Music Education devoted a number of pages to the notion that studying music contributes to success in school and in life (National Association for Music Education, 1991). In the middle and late 1990s, many people were justifying music based on the "Mozart effect," in which listening to Mozart's music appeared to temporarily help students in terms of spatial reasoning.

Why has music been so persistently justified on nonmusical grounds? Is it because those beliefs are true? Is it because music educators need practical reasons to establish a case for music in the schools? Or do they think nonmusical reasons are more easily understood by people who are not musicians than a "quality of life" explanation? The answer is, "All of the above." But the matter is not a simple one.

Music can contribute much to other areas of the curriculum, and this should happen more often than it currently does in the schools.

However, usually the use of nonmusical values to justify music is more concerned with effects on individual students and with something more than music's psychological value and the enrichment it can offer other school subjects.

Claims that something automatically transfers from music to other areas of curriculum or life are often exaggerated. To begin with, the variations in types of instruction in music make a great deal of difference. Musical sounds in and of themselves do not increase intelligence, help people to negotiate disagreements, or aid in preventing illnesses. Karen Wolff (1978) carefully analyzed the available research on the transfer of learning in music to other subjects. She found specific transfer only in language arts and some inadequate studies that indicate there may be some other positive benefits of music study. Some benefits have also been observed in improved attitudes toward school on the part of students as indicated by a decline in absenteeism (Rodosky, 1974). Some of this benefit may happen because music offers the students a refreshing change from what they usually do in school. Music can be an effective "anti-monotony" activity.

There is some additional intriguing evidence about music and success in school—and presumably then in life. Students who participate in music generally score higher on Scholastic Aptitude Tests (SAT) than students who are not in any arts courses. In 2001, the music students in performing groups bettered the non-arts students by 57 points (out of a possible 800 points) in the verbal measure and 41 in the quantitative measure (Princeton University, 2001). Another study found that children given piano lessons significantly improved in their spatial temporal IQ scores compared to children who received computer lessons, casual singing, or no lessons (Rauscher et al., 1997, pp. 1–8).

On the surface, these results would seem to prove once and for all that music has direct mental benefits beyond its artistic ones. Maybe. Music is good for people, but results such as higher SAT scores do not prove that music *causes* music students to be smarter. It could be that the smarter students gravitate toward music, which often is the case. It is very difficult to separate cause (why something happened) from correlation (two events related by time or place). For example, in one high school, three of the five boys on the tennis team were National Merit finalists. Did playing tennis make them more intelligent, or were the more academic-type students attracted to tennis? Very likely it was the latter reason.

Although it is nearly impossible to prove in a controlled study, some students acquire what might be called a "cycle of success" in which already able and alert students are involved with music. In turn, this involvement helps them to become even more able to be winners. Whether this cycle of success is the result of attitude, ability, or hard work doesn't matter. One accomplishment seems to fuel another, and for many high school students, music is an important area of accomplishment.

In making a case for music, music educators need to keep four facts in mind:

1. The research evidence supporting most claims of nonmusical value is limited to language development, spatial reasoning, and attitude toward school.

2. Some of the available research is of questionable quality.

3. Many nonmusical benefits can be achieved better in areas other than music; e.g., good citizenship is usually studied better in social science classes.

4. Nonmusical claims tend to divert attention from the fact that music merits serious study, regardless of any nonmusical benefits. Biology teachers, for example, do not claim they teach something more than knowledge of biology and the scientific method, and music does not need to make such claims either.

There are many personal benefits from participation in music activities—performing before an audience, getting to know a teacher who is a good role model, achieving recognition in terms of an award, and so on. Such benefits are also available in other extracurricular activities. Some students find success in special clubs, others in athletics, others with the school paper, and others in music.

The avocational value of music becomes significant after students have completed high school. While the average life expectancy has increased, the average workweek has decreased. These facts mean that more time for leisure time is available to people. Music is an important avocational activity in many countries. In North America alone, the membership of the League of American Orchestras (2017) includes more than 2,000 organizations and individuals, and there are thousands of church choirs and other amateur choral groups.

Two important points should be remembered about the nonmusical outcomes of music instruction:

1. There are valid and supportable reasons for including music in the curricula of all schools apart from any nonmusical benefits. The nonmusical benefits should be thought of as bonuses for instruction that the schools should offer anyway. The place of

music in schools does not depend on them, but its position may be stronger because of them.

2. There is usually little a teacher can do directly to make these psychological and avocational benefits happen. The self-image of students, their social and psychological needs, and their choices of what to do with their time after school are all influenced by circumstances over which teachers have little control. Teachers cannot use a teaching procedure that ensures any non-musical benefits, although good teaching can help create a situation in which they are more likely to be realized.

STUDENTS OR THE SUBJECT?

The fact that students can learn the subject of music while gaining personal and social benefits should lay to rest a long-standing but false dilemma: Should teachers teach the subject or the students? The answer is they should teach both. It's not an either-or proposition. Students are not helped if they are left ignorant about what they should know, no matter what their personal situations may be. On the other hand, teachers cannot ignore that they teach human beings. They need to be flexible and sensitive to the students' needs so they can do the best teaching job possible.

To voice its feelings about the value of teaching music, the NAfME developed a statement music teachers can use to remind themselves about the value and importance of their work (see Figure 1.1).

QUESTIONS

1. In what ways do people show that they value music?
2. Why can't most young people just learn music on their own without needing music instruction in school?
3. What are the characteristics of aesthetic experiences?
4. Why don't music educators need to establish the fact that music has some nonmusical values in order to justify its place in the schools?
5. In what ways does music appear to have much potential for several nonmusical benefits?
6. What would most students miss if they did not receive music instruction in school?

Figure 1.1   Music Educators' Creed

Music Educators' Creed

As a music teacher, I devote myself to two important causes:

1. Helping all people to make music a part of their lives, and
2. Advancing the art of music.

I believe that all people have the right to an education in music that:

- teaches them the lifelong joy of making music through singing and playing instruments
- gives them a chance to express through music what cannot be expressed in words
- helps them to respond to music intellectually and emotionally
- teaches them the language of music notation and opens the door to improvising, composing, and arranging
- equips them to make informed judgments about musical works and performances
- educates them in the music of all cultures and historical eras
- allows them to discover and develop their special talents, including preparing to make music their profession, if they so choose
- prepares them to be involved with music throughout their lives

I teach music because—music makes a difference in the lives of people.

Music Educators' Creed developed by Music Educators National Conference, 1991.
Source: *Soundpost*, 8 (3) (Spring 1992), p. 9.

PROJECTS

1. Write a brief paragraph (100 words or less) stating why you think music should be taught in schools.
2. Ask two persons who are currently teaching music in schools to describe a few instances that helped convince them of the value of music classes and groups. Report your findings to the class.

REFERENCES

Barry, N., Taylor, J., Walls, K., & Wood, J. (1990). *The role of the fine and performing arts in high school dropout prevention.* Tallahassee: Florida State University.

Birge, F. B. (1966). *The history of public school music in the United States.* Reston, VA: Music Educators National Conference.

Dykema, P. W., & Gehrkens, K. (1941). *The teaching and administration of high school music.* Evanston, IL: Summy-Burchard.

League of American Orchestras. (2017). *About the league.* Accessed from www.americanorchestras.org/about-the-league.html

National Association for Music Education (NAfME). (1991). *Growing up complete: The imperative for music education. The Report of the National Commission on Music Education.* New York: Rowman & Littlefield.

Princeton University. (2001). *College-bound seniors national report: Profile of SAT program test takers.* Princeton, NJ: The College Entrance Examination Board.

Rauscher, F. H., Shaw, G. L., Levine, L. J., Wright, E. L., Dennis, W. R., & Newcomb, R. (1997). Music training causes long-term enhancement of preschool children's spatial temporal reasoning. *Neurological Research, 19,* 1–8.

Rodosky, R. (1974). *Arts IMPACT final evaluation report.* Columbus, OH: Columbus Public Schools.

Wolff, K. (1978). The nonmusical outcomes of music education: A review of the literature. *Council of Research in Music Education,* Bulletin 55.

The Nature of
Teaching Music

Where do we start in becoming more able to analyze what music teachers do? A good place is with having a clear understanding about what the words "music" and "teach" mean. Although their meanings may seem obvious, both have implications that are basic to what music teachers do, or at least what they should do.

WHAT IS MUSIC?

The nature of music seems like a simple matter, but is it? Is the crash of a cymbal or an eerie sound from an electronic instrument music? Why is a boom from a bass drum considered musical and booms from thunder thought of as noise? The difference is not so much in the sounds themselves as it is in the context in which they are heard. If they appear in an organized sequence of sounds, they become music; if not, they are just random noises. The key to the matter is organization. In fact, music has often been defined as organized sound.

Organizing sounds in a span of time is something that human beings do. Music is not preordained by the cosmic laws of the universe, and therefore something that people uncover. Instead it is created by humans for humans. It is a human activity, and it varies in the forms it takes, just as other human creations such as language, clothing, and food vary.

The world of music is vast and complex. Not only does it include all the music that has been created—folk, symphonic, instrumental, vocal, electronic, rock—it also encompasses musical activities such as singing, listening, analyzing, and creating. In fact, music is both a *product* in terms of being composed or improvised and a *process* in terms of the actions involved in producing or reproducing music.

The vastness of the world of music forces teachers to make choices about what to teach and how to teach it. Fortunately, the definition of music as organized sound offers a clue to the most important responsibility of music teachers: guiding students to understand and appreciate organized sounds. The processes of performing and creating music often help in achieving this goal. For example, creating melodies gives students an understanding of organizing sounds, and so does singing or playing melodies on a clarinet.

Sometimes teachers emphasize one aspect of music so much that other aspects are largely ignored. Some teachers, for example, concentrate so much on the techniques of singing, playing, or creating music that the students never get around to understanding where that activity fits into the world of music. In other cases, teachers devote so much attention to factual information that the students fail to think of music as an artistic experience.

Successful music teaching requires a balanced view of the world of music. It also requires careful decisions, because time for music is almost always limited. Both musical objects and processes are needed, as is variety in the type of music students study. And both information and activities should be related to organized sounds.

What Is Teaching?

Teaching is the organizing and guiding of a process in which students learn. Simply put, the role of teachers is to bring about the acquisition of information, understanding, and skills on the part of their students. The way in which this task is accomplished can take a number of different forms. Sometimes it consists of providing the students with information, while at other times it involves setting up a learning situation and then stepping aside as the students work on their own. In some instances, it means deciding on assignments for students to do individually; in other cases, it consists of leading a group in a unified effort such as singing a song. Whatever form teaching takes, the essential result is that students learn. That is what the process of teaching is all about, not the particular actions teachers take when working with students. The essential goal of teaching should not be confused with its different styles.

The definition of teaching as a process in which students learn also has implications for the attributes of teachers. Although a teacher may exhibit charm and good looks, lecture brilliantly, manage a classroom well, and use this or that method, if little learning takes place, he or she has not been successful as a teacher. In fact, occasionally (but not typically) a person who appears to violate the usual assumptions about what is needed to be a good teacher turns out to be highly effective in getting students to learn. Teaching is so subtle and complex an endeavor that such a situation can happen every so often.

Because it is subtle and complex, a teacher is more effective with some students than with others, no matter how hard they may try to reach every student. Each student brings different abilities, interests, and background to a class or rehearsal. The chemistry between an individual student and a teacher is never the same with all the students. No teacher bats 1,000 in effectiveness with any class or group.

Teachers' jobs usually include duties in addition to leading the learning-teaching process—checking out instruments, taking attendance, keeping order in the classroom, and so on. Most of these duties are important and necessary, but they are not really part of the teaching–learning process. A person can be a good classroom manager and still not be an effective teacher.

ANALYZING MUSIC TEACHING

Whether they realize it or not, almost all successful teachers have learned to think about teaching in an analytical way. They have an approach to the process. When all is said and done, teaching comes down to a few simple but basic components that can be stated as questions:

- *Why* teach music?
- *What* should be taught?
- *How* will it be taught?
- *To whom* will it be taught?
- *With what results?*

Each component is discussed in later chapters, but the following is a brief overview of each part of the process.

Why Teach Music?

The most basic question concerns why music needs to be taught. That's why it is the topic of the initial chapters in this book. The answer to that question provides teachers with a sense of direction, and to a degree it affects the answers to the other four questions. Teachers who lack a clear understanding of what they are about are like rudderless ships floundering on the seas of education.

Fortunately, it is not necessary to return to the question of "why?" when thinking about every class or rehearsal. If you can express your reasons for teaching music, it will give direction and consistency to your teaching. However, from time to time it is a good idea to rethink the fundamental reasons for teaching music. Maturity, experience, and changed circumstances call for periodic review of your views. The topic is too important to be decided once and for all at the age of twenty. Develop some solid answers now to the question of why music should be taught, but don't chisel your beliefs in stone this early in your career.

What Should Be Taught in Music?

The content of music classes deals with the "stuff" of music—musical works, facts, fingerings, patterns of sound, understanding of the process of creating music, interpretation, and similar things. It includes all types of information, skills, and attitudes, and it should also light the spark of creativity and individual expression within students.

Deciding what to teach is a complex matter. The world of music is huge, which makes choices about what to teach really difficult. Other factors also contribute to the complexity of making these decisions, including practical considerations such as the musical background of the students, the amount of time available, the traditions of the community, the size of the class, and the amount and type of materials available or required in a districtwide or statewide curriculum.

Music teachers should also remember that students learn not just in music classes or under the guidance of teachers. After all, students spend only about 1,000 of the 8,736 hours of their lives each year in school, so it is not reasonable to credit or blame the school for everything they can or cannot do. The fact remains, however, that only a very limited amount of learning about music usually takes place without organized, competent instruction.

Unlike the question of why, the matter of what to teach needs to be spelled out specifically for each lesson or class. There should always be clearly stated objectives in terms of what the students are to learn.

How Should Music Be Taught?

The question of how music is taught focuses on ways of organizing and structuring instruction, as well as selecting the manner of presentation. Some people who have never taught falsely assume that teaching is a job in which a teacher merely stands in front of students and talks. If that were the case, teaching would indeed be easy! However, that's not the way it is, even if some experienced teachers make it look easy.

The suggestions in methods textbooks are geared to what might be considered typical situations. Readers should realize, however, that there are almost no typical schools. Each school is unique, just as each student is unique. The ideas presented in books and classes apply to a majority of teaching situations. As much as an author would like to, it is impossible to offer specific ideas on how to teach music in each of the thousands of schools in the United States.

The difficulty in specifying procedures for all situations is not characteristic of other professions. For example, because nearly everyone's appendix is in approximately the same part of the body, surgeons are taught a specific surgical procedure for its removal. Unfortunately, human behavior is much less consistent than human anatomy. Very few students have the same interests, musical background, and mental ability. For this reason, identical teaching procedures sometimes produce the opposite results in different classrooms, especially when different teachers are involved. Part of the challenge of teaching is being adaptable and resourceful enough to meet a variety of situations.

Deciding on which methods are most appropriate for teaching specific material to a particular group of students is one of the challenges of teaching. Suppose a teacher wishes to teach a second grade class to sing a song with pleasing tone and accurate pitch. Because the song is simple, it presents the teacher with no technical obstacles. The children are enjoyable to work with and tractable, offering the teacher few problems in guiding the class. The challenge comes in presenting the song so that it becomes meaningful to seven-year-old youngsters. How can the contour of the melodic line be impressed on children who don't know what the word "contour" means? How does a teacher make second graders conscious of accurate pitches when they sing? How can phrases of the song be presented so the students will understand better the function of a phrase? Does a gentle sweep of the arm really aid children in perceiving phrases, or are there other means that might be more effective? These questions only scratch the surface of the depth of the challenges involved in teaching a simple song.

A sizable amount of information exists about learning and the conditions under which it takes place. This available information should be the "stuff" of music methods courses. Ideas on teaching change as new information and the means of presenting it become available from technology, research, and practical experience. For example, it was once believed that language reading should be introduced by teaching letters of the alphabet first, since words are made up of letters. When the alphabet was learned, it was put into words and finally into sentences (Swaby, 1984). This method, known as the ABC method, seems logical, but what is considered logical is not always the way people function. Today, teachers know that words are comprehended as a whole, not letter by letter. Without this knowledge and without training in how to use it, teachers can waste much time and introduce habits that will have to be broken later. A fluent reading ability and a gracious way with children are not sufficient qualifications for teaching reading. The same is true of teaching music.

To Whom Is Music Being Taught?

The capabilities and motivation of the students are essential components in the teaching process. Not only must teachers consider such obvious matters as the range of voices and previous musical knowledge, but they should also be aware of the probable use the students will make of what they learn. A fifth-grade general music class and a high school choir may both study the same folk song, but each will approach it in a different way and with different degrees of technical information.

The "To whom?" question requires that teachers put themselves in the place of the students in order to recognize better their varied interests, needs, and backgrounds. Teachers should try to see the subject through the eyes of their students. This ability is needed not only to know how to adapt methods and materials, but also to establish a teacher–class relationship that will encourage a positive attitude in the students. They are often slow to distinguish between their feelings about the teacher and their feelings about the subject. And in a subject such as music, in which so much depends on feeling and perception, the students' attitudes are especially important. When students realize that the teacher is sensitive to their interests, the relationship between pupils and teacher is really improved and more learning takes place.

With What Results?

The fifth component in the teaching process is finding out the results of a class or lesson. Teachers should assess to what extent the objectives of a class or rehearsal were accomplished. It is easy for teachers to assume that because they covered a point, the students have learned it. Maybe they have, but maybe they haven't. The best way to find out how much students have learned is to have at least a representative sample of them respond individually to questions or perform a short passage. Listening to a group perform a song or instrumental piece provides information about the group, which is useful but limited in terms of what individual students have accomplished. One good bass in a choir can easily cover up the fact that most of the basses really haven't learned their part.

The objectives for a lesson or rehearsal and the assessment of the students' accomplishment of those objectives are two sides of the same coin, so to speak. Unless objectives are stated clearly, assessment is virtually impossible. Teaching without assessing is like driving in a strange city without a map or GPS; you may make it to your destination, but some luck will be needed to do so.

"Rehearse 'He watching over Israel' at letter C" is not a clear or adequately stated objective. Why? Because it says nothing about what the students are to learn from rehearsing at letter C. Instead, "Each section will sing its part at letter C with a clear tone, accurate pitch, and proper expression" is assessable, although some judgments will be required about what is a clear tone, accurate pitch, and correct expression.

What is needed is evidence in terms of what students can do as a result of the learning experience. The term "observable behavior" does not refer to classroom deportment, although there is some relationship between the quality of teaching and classroom conduct. Instead, it refers to what was learned as revealed through the students' abilities to answer questions, to signal when a theme returns, to sing or play the third of a triad when asked, or to add an improvised phrase to a line of music.

Why? What? How? To whom? With what results? The answers to these questions are the essential parts of the process called teaching. If teachers fail to think through each one of these questions, they run the risk of producing educational failures marked by wasted time and lost opportunities for learning. Teaching is similar in this respect to getting an airplane off the ground. If any important part is missing or not working, the plane will not take off. Because educational failures are less dramatic and less immediately visible than airplanes failing to become airborne, some teachers are able to hold their jobs without thinking carefully about what they are doing. Only their students are the losers! Sometimes the material is too difficult, too easy, or meaningless; sometimes the hours spent in music classes add up to little additional knowledge or skills for the students; sometimes teachers and classes wander, not knowing what they are trying to accomplish or if the students have learned anything. When any of these situations occurs, it is an educational failure.

The five components provide an approach for thinking and learning about teaching. They also give focus to thoughts that could otherwise be a formless blob in one's mind.

Figure 2.1   Components of the Teaching Process

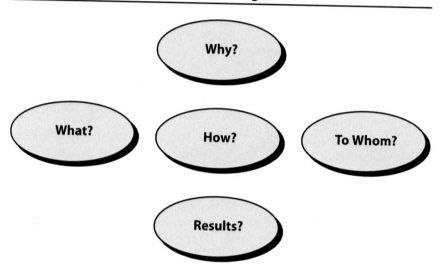

OBSERVING MUSIC TEACHING

A logical first step in thinking analytically about teaching is for you to observe music classes and analyze what teachers do. This chapter contains a practice analysis form for a music class that you are probably taking now (see Figure 2.2).

Figure 2.3 on page 24 presents a more extensive form for you to use when observing music teachers in school situations. Both forms focus attention on what teachers do. At this point in preparing to be a teacher, you should *not* be rendering general judgments about teachers! Before you can do that in any meaningful way, you need to be able to look systematically at what teachers do.

Figure 2.2   On-Campus Observation Form

On-Campus Observation Form

Most of you have the good fortune to be taking a music theory and/or a music history course. Since you are attending this class anyway, it is a convenient one for gaining skill in analyzing the teaching process (not the instructor!). Select only *one* class (not the entire course) from either of these areas for this assignment. Analyze the teaching process by answering the following five questions:

1. Why? What is the reason for this course and the material covered in the particular class?

2. What? What specifically are the students in the class supposed to be learning?

3. How? What method or methods is the instructor using to teach the content to the students?

4. To whom? What appear to be the musical backgrounds and interests of the students in the class?

5. Results? What actions, if any, did the instructor take to determine how well the students had learned what was being taught? If such actions were taken, how well did it appear that the students had learned?

Figure 2.3 Off-Campus Observation Form for Practice Analysis

Off-Campus Observation Form

Student's name:
Teacher observed:
School:
Date of observation:
Type of class observed:
Age or grade of students:

What appeared to be the objectives of the class?

How did the teacher try to achieve those objectives?

How did the students respond to the teaching procedures?

What methods of classroom control did you observe?

How well were the objectives of the class accomplished?

What did you particularly like about what the teacher did in teaching the class?

What would you try to do differently if you had been the teacher of the class?

Other information or thoughts:

QUESTIONS

1. What makes some groups of sounds music and other groups of sounds noise?
2. What five questions make up the basic components of the teaching process?
3. Why is it impossible to spell out in advance the exact procedures for teaching music to any class?
4. In what ways is music both a product and a process?

Planning and Assessing Music Teaching

3

The reasons for planning to teach any subject may be so obvious that they are sometimes forgotten. The main reason for planning is to enable teachers to know what they want to accomplish and how they will accomplish it. There are also other benefits of planning. One is the feeling of confidence and security it encourages, which usually helps a teacher be more effective. Another benefit of planning is that time and effort are not wasted because of uncertainty and confusion in front of a class.

Assessing the amount and quality of what the students in a class or ensemble have learned provides guidance for teachers in considering what they should plan for in subsequent classes or rehearsals. It takes some of the guesswork out of what they should incorporate in the future.

AMOUNT OF PLANNING BY MUSIC TEACHERS

Many music teachers, especially those who direct performing groups, do not appear to do much planning. In fact, a few teachers seem to do none at all, except for setting some performance dates and attending to other nonteaching matters. If planning has the benefits just described, then why don't all music teachers, including those who teach performing groups, do more of it?

There are several likely reasons. One is that some music teachers think the function of music groups is to entertain the students. Learning does not matter all that much to them as long as the students seem content. Some teachers wonder if anyone cares whether the students in their classes learn much. The rewards for teachers for actually teaching their students music are often not very strong in terms of public recognition.

In addition, many music teachers carry a heavy teaching load. They hurry from one class to the next for six hours a day, and after school they have special rehearsals or they help students individually or in small ensembles. Often there is little time or energy left for planning at the end of the day.

There are, furthermore, aspects of music teaching that simply cannot be fully planned. When teaching a song in two parts to a general music class, it is hard to know how well the students will learn something. Therefore, music teachers must make some on-the-spot decisions regardless of the amount of prior planning.

Finally, a few music teachers are suspicious of planning because they feel it might interfere with their flexibility and spontaneity in the classroom. This might be true if teachers were unwilling to make any changes in their plans and allow their plans to shackle their enthusiasm and adaptability. Clearly, if it seems wise to alter a plan and it appears that the students will learn more if a change is made, then no teacher should hesitate to change what has been planned. Although some plans may be altered before they are used, the original planning is never a waste of time. The unused planning can be a foundation on which a teacher can build a better lesson in the future. It can provide something to work from, which is better than stumbling along without objectives and ideas about how best to achieve them.

Aids in Planning

It is not a sign of weakness or incompetence to take advantage of books and curriculum guides in planning, especially when you are not an experienced teacher. Music teachers in secondary schools sometimes have five classes a day, and elementary music specialists often teach music at six different grade levels and meet each class just once a week. These limited amounts of teaching time require careful planning. To make matters more difficult, a beginning teacher has no reservoir of ideas and experience, so even greater efforts in planning are needed.

Long-Range Planning

Where does a teacher start in planning for an entire school year? Because this is no easy task, the beginning teacher should feel free to take ideas from any source—books, curriculum guides, and other teachers. But what kind of ideas? The answer: Ideas about what he or she wants the students to learn or be able to do.

In the beginning, these ideas will probably be quite general. They will need to be honed and sharpened and then stated clearly in terms of student actions. For example, suppose you would like to see the students understand and read music notation better. That is a good but general notion. The next step is to state the idea in specific terms so you can express more clearly what you want them to know about or do with notation. It might be that you want them to become conscious of the size of intervals in a melody. You hope they notice that adjacent intervals sound closer than wide intervals, and you also hope that the students can identify the basic intervals such as thirds and fifths when they see or hear them. What began as a general guide has now become more specific.

Although it may not be easy to fill in the blanks for classes meeting a couple of months in the future, teachers should attempt to plan for an entire semester or school year. Long-term planning allows for thinking through the sequence in which topics will be presented. Without such plans, gaps or duplication may occur.

Unit Planning

In a sense, planning for a group of classes or rehearsals is halfway between planning for an entire course and planning for just one class. Unit plans have elements of long-term planning in that they cover three or more classes, but they are much more specific about what will be taught and how it will be taught. Sometimes plans for a small number of classes or rehearsals can be written at the same time. The idea of unit planning makes it possible for a topic to be a unifying thread for a number of classes. A topic is not treated in just one short presentation. Rather, it is developed and studied in enough depth to help the students remember it better.

Because class situations vary so much, and because each unit for a general music class has its own particular requirements, it is impossible to provide a model plan that can be used for all units. Basically, the unit should focus on some phase of music and integrate as much as possible the activities of singing, listening, creating, discussing, and reading. It is neither possible nor desirable for every unit to encompass in one class period the wide variety of activities that could be included. Some topics suggest singing, while others invite discussion and study. When possible, videos, books, computer materials, field trips, and appearances by outside authorities should be integrated into the unit of study as logical extensions of the learning experience.

The rehearsals of performing groups can also be planned in units. If, as is hoped, the rehearsal consists of more than preparing for one public performance after another, then units can be formed around types of music, forms, or technical problems. For example, a unit for studying choral music could be created about the characteristics of works from Russia or the Renaissance, a unit of band music developed around overtures, and a unit for orchestra created around types of bowing. While such learning is going on, the group is also rehearsing the music for performance.

Lesson Planning

Lesson planning is merely the process of organizing the things that a particular class will do. Although several approaches can be used to develop lesson plans, certain guidelines should be considered:

1. Determine as much as possible where the students are in terms of the subject and what has been covered in previous classes. Then, think of what would be worthwhile for them to learn in music. Finding out the students' present knowledge or skills may involve giving a short test or it can be a general group assessment of their performing level. Furthermore, after a teacher has taught a group of students for a while, he or she should have a much clearer idea about what the students know and can do.

2. Select two or three specific topics or skills to teach, or one specific topic or skill in each class or rehearsal. Students, especially those in elementary and middle school, become restless and their attention wanes if any one activity is continued for too long a time. One activity is satisfactory for rehearsals because a lot of time is spent playing or singing, but the music being rehearsed needs to change every ten to fifteen minutes.

3. State the points to be studied specifically. An objective such as "to learn about music composed in the Renaissance style" is too vague and too broad. An objective such as "to identify aurally and in notation the points of imitation in Renaissance madrigals and motets" is much clearer and more manageable.

4. State the objectives for the class or group in terms of what the students should be able to do as a result of the instruction. Unless students can provide evidence of how much they have

learned, it is more difficult for a teacher to determine what should be taught in subsequent classes. Objectives can apply to skills as well as to information. For example, "The group will learn to sing Palestrina's *Sanctus* with a light tone and accurate pitch." Other objectives can apply to learning with a criterion level added if the teacher so desires. For example, "Ninety percent of the students will be able to locate three examples of imitative entrances in the notation of *Sanctus* by Palestrina."

5. Select appropriate materials. Teachers who wish to teach about Renaissance madrigals should try to secure the most authentic version of each madrigal that is available and play recordings of madrigals being sung in an authentic style.

6. Decide how the content is to be taught. Suppose that an elementary school class is learning to identify A-B-A form. There are several ways in which this could be done. If the class knows a song that is in A-B-A form, they could sing it through and identify the different sections. A recording of a work with clearly delineated sections in A-B-A could be played. Or the students could create a simple piece in three-part form using classroom instruments. They might think of ways to represent visually the different sections of a piece of music, such as with different symbols or colors for the various sections of the work. Each of these ways—and many others—are appropriate under the right circumstances.

7. Assess the results of each portion of a class or rehearsal. Teachers need to gather evidence on how well the students have learned what was taught.

You will be given experiences in creating lesson plans in the methods courses you take as you approach student teaching. The format will be specified by the instructor, so it is not possible to provide a model. However, they should be based on the five basic questions covered in Chapter 2 that constitute the teaching process.

Planning for Rehearsals

To prepare for rehearsals, teachers must decide which pieces will be studied, which places in each work should receive special attention, and what should be learned in conjunction with the work. For example, if a chorus is singing an arrangement of a Mexican folk song, the students should learn about features, such as parallel thirds, that contribute to its musical character.

In addition, teachers need to study the scores for works they don't already know, practice any special conducting techniques, and decide how they should be interpreted. Also, their study should anticipate places that are likely to be troublesome for the ensemble. When students reach a difficult passage, the teacher must quickly be able to come up with suggestions such as the alternative fingering for G on the trumpet, a bowing technique that will help the strings coordinate the bow with the left hand, or a suggestion for getting the woodwinds to play a particular rhythmic figure correctly.

No single outline of activity is suitable for all rehearsals of performing groups. Methods and content should vary according to what the students have learned previously, the closeness of a performance, and the type of music being studied. Many teachers begin rehearsals with a combination warm-up and technique-developing routine. This portion of the rehearsal should be varied from day to day and be relevant to other activities in the course. In singing, for example, attention can be centered on producing the sound correctly or singing in tune. In instrumental music, playing techniques can be stressed, or a scale or exercise can be played to practice correct fingerings or bowings. Warm-up activity should be brief—no longer than five minutes.

To close a rehearsal, students can review a piece of music they do well or put together something on which they have been working. The idea is to avoid leaving the group hanging in the middle of a piece of music or activity when the rehearsal ends. Between its opening and closing the group can begin studying new music, review familiar works, perfect its current repertoire, or learn aspects of music theory and literature relevant to the music being rehearsed.

ASSESSING LEARNING IN MUSIC

Planning and assessment are two aspects of teaching that are closely related. In fact, assessment is not even possible unless the objectives have been clearly stated. As the saying goes, "If you don't know where you're going, you can never tell if you have gotten there."

Why is it important for teachers to assess what their students have learned? Teachers need to have some information about how well the students have achieved the objectives. Without such knowledge, teachers are forced to rely on impressions, hunches, and assumptions. At least by observing what students can do, teachers will not continue to be ineffective due to a lack of information about what their students learned in a class or rehearsal.

A second reason for assessing learning is the observable evidence of learning that it can provide. It is impossible to observe directly what students know or think. Therefore, teachers must consider the actions of students such as answering questions or demonstrating skills based on what they were taught.

A third reason for assessing learning is that it can lead to more valid grading of students.

Assessing the effectiveness of instruction does not mean giving one test after another. Nor is it necessary to involve all the members of a class or ensemble in every evaluation. A random sample of four or five students selected to answer questions or in other ways indicate what they are learning is usually enough to provide teachers with a good idea of how much learning took place.

Although they contain many features in common, testing and assessing have somewhat different purposes. Tests are generally related to grading students. Test questions need to be representative of the material covered in class. Tests also need to be worded clearly and have clearly correct answers. The manner and importance of grading students is a complex issue that educators have been debating for at least the last 75 years. The nature of a test varies widely according to grade level and subject matter.

The assessment of student learning has a different purpose. It seeks to provide teachers with information regarding the nature and extent of what the students have learned. Armed with the information assessment provides, teachers can then improve future lessons on similar topics. It's a fact: teachers are largely responsible for making themselves into successful teachers. The assessment of classes, with the resulting improvements that they encourage, are a very important means of growing and improving as a music teacher.

Assessment of classes may sound like a lot of work. It isn't. Whereas testing usually involves all students in a class, assessing needs to include only a representative sample of students, perhaps less than one fourth of them. The purpose is to gather a solid impression of what students appear to have learned in a class or lesson. To help make an assessment more valid, both strong and weak students need to be involved, not just those who raise their hands and show more interest in the class.

Questions

1. Why is it difficult for instructors and authors of educational materials to specify in detail the procedures for teaching music to all fifth grade classes?

2. What is an observable behavior? Why are observable behaviors so important in analyzing the teaching process?

3. What are the benefits to music teachers, including directors of performing groups, of planning for their classes and rehearsals?

4. What are the advantages of unit planning?

5. What factors should music teachers consider when planning for a class or rehearsal?

6. What are the benefits of assessing the results of music classes and rehearsals?

7. What is the main difference between testing and assessing?

Project

Think of a song or piece of music that music teachers typically teach a class or performing group. Next, imagine a class or group to which to you can teach an aspect of that piece of music. Then, answer the following questions:

- Why is it useful for students to learn that fact or skill?

- Precisely, what about that aspect of music are the students to learn?

- How would that fact or skill be taught to the group of students you have in mind?

- How would you determine how well the students have learned?

Qualities and Competencies of Music Teachers

4

Are people born with the ability to teach music well, or do they become good teachers through hard work and self-improvement? What characteristics do most good music teachers possess? Where do pre-professional experiences and student teaching fit into the training of teachers? These and other questions are concerned with the type of persons music teachers should be, the skills and knowledge they need to possess, and the ways in which they can continue to improve their ability to teach after they get a job. Because music programs can be no stronger than the people who function in carrying them out, the qualities and abilities of music teachers are vitally important.

One purpose of an introductory course in music education is to encourage you to think about what constitutes a good music teacher. Some of what is involved concerns actions music teachers take, while part of it involves the personal qualities and attributes of teachers.

PERSONALITY

Research and writings on the topic of the personality of good teachers have tended to reaffirm what nearly everyone already knows: warm, friendly, understanding teachers are more effective than those who aren't. Businesslike and organized teachers are more effective than those who are careless and disorganized. Imaginative and enthusiastic teachers are more successful than those who are routine and dull.

A few points can be stated with confidence, however, about the personality of successful music teachers. They need to be adults in the fullest sense of the word, and they should be conscious of the needs and feelings of others. The whims and idiosyncrasies of an artistic temperament have no place in the schools.

It does seem that music teachers are susceptible to greater personal involvement in their work than are most other teachers. Consider their background. They have often been involved in competitive contests since they were in middle school, auditions for chairs in ensembles, and regular juries in college. All these experiences required an above-average amount of self-reliance and mental toughness. Certainly elementary classroom teachers and teachers of other academic subjects have not had to deal with such demanding situations. Furthermore, music teachers who direct ensembles have their names on programs and often take their ensembles for auditions in which their performance is rated. A teacher's success is frequently equated with the amount of attention their ensembles achieve. An ensemble and a director's recognition are often linked together.

Whatever the reasons, quite a few directors of ensembles tend to view their work as an extension of themselves. For example, a number of times I have heard music teachers tell almost boastfully how the choir or band "fell apart" after they left a particular teaching position. Some teachers work hard with students who have above-average ability because they help bring recognition to the teacher. On the other hand, they have little time for less talented students.

Music teachers need to be aware that pressures for personal involvement will be present throughout their teaching careers, especially for those who teach ensembles What they need to do—and do often—is remind themselves that teachers achieve their satisfaction from observing the learning of their students. Music exists in the schools for the benefit of the students, not the teachers.

The preceding paragraph about the satisfactions in teaching may sound like a teacher's role is one of self-sacrifice. Wrong! It's not so much a sacrifice of self as it is a different way of achieving satisfaction. When you teach so that the students learn something they would not have learned without your efforts, it is truly gratifying. There is something deeply rewarding when you realize that you are making a difference in the lives of people, especially young people. Such satisfaction can hardly be thought of as a "sacrifice."

The grooming and appearance of teachers is a subject that has occasionally produced lively discussions, but it probably has little effect on how much students learn, as long as it does not detract from or interfere with the respect and confidence the students have in the teacher. It is everyone's personal right as a citizen to wear whatever hairdo or clothing style they wish. But if a person's appearance causes students to consider the teacher as strange or odd, then it is not worth the loss of learning that results. Each school has its own standards, both written and unwritten, on this matter. New teachers should err on the side of dressing conservatively for the first few days until they know better what is expected in terms of ties, shoes, and other clothing.

The speaking voice of teachers should be pleasing and, more important, should carry a quality of decisiveness. During student teaching, the complaint sometimes leveled at a novice teacher is that he or she can scarcely be heard in the back of the room. The problem usually disappears as the beginning teacher gains confidence and experience and makes an effort to improve in this area.

In the final analysis, there is a quality beyond what is visible: a sense of commitment to being a good teacher. David Ausubel, a noted educational psychologist, wrote:

> Perhaps the most important personality characteristic of a teacher . . . [is] . . . the extent of the teacher's personal commitment to the intellectual development of students. . . . It determines in large measure whether he will expend the necessary effort to teach for real gains in the intellectual growth of pupils or will merely go through the formal motions of teaching. (Ausubel, Novak, and Hanesian, 1978)

Myron Brenton (1970) is more blunt: "The best teachers wear a large invisible button that reads, 'I give a damn.'"

THE IMPORTANCE OF BEING YOURSELF

When authors or committees write about what teachers should be like, they are presenting an ideal or model, not a set of minimum competencies that must be met. They realize teachers are human beings, and that no one can fulfill every suggested quality. The reason that many qualities are mentioned here is to make readers aware of what is desirable.

Every one of us has strong and weak points in terms of being a teacher. It is obvious that we should use our strengths to the fullest in order to compensate for weaker points. With some teachers, their strength may be their ability to play the piano; with others it may be their ability to inspire students or their knowledge of music. Each person develops different ways to fulfill the role of teacher. Figure 4.1 contains a form that will help you appraise your strengths and weaknesses as a prospective music educator. Complete the form, even if you never show it to anyone.

Many young teachers who have performed under a dynamic, extroverted individual or observed such a person in full swing at a workshop may wonder, "Is it necessary for me to have that kind of personality to be successful?" Extroversion does not guarantee a teacher's ability to convey ideas and teach effectively. Suppose a teacher puts on a red shirt and conducts like a cheerleader. At first, it would probably grab the attention of the students. But what about the fiftieth or hundredth class? What was once attention-grabbing could become downright annoying.

Many good music teachers are not extroverts and would look silly if they pretended to be. Instead of extroversion, what is needed is a quality of decisiveness, of knowing what you are teaching, and letting the students know you are competent and in charge. Good teachers cannot be weak and timid. The ways in which each individual achieves this quality of competence depends on his or her unique personality, but it must be achieved, especially with secondary school ensembles. Two conditions help to give the impression of competence: (1) a firm belief that what you are teaching is worth the students' knowing, and (2) the confidence that arises from understanding what you are about as a teacher. Beyond these basic understandings the quality of decisiveness is something that many future teachers need to work on and develop through experience.

HUMAN QUALITIES AND PROFESSIONAL COMPETENCE

It is easy to point out that teachers should be sensible, fair, decisive, and interested in students' learning. But how do these attributes relate to the ability of teachers to work with people, something that is central to teaching? Here are some thoughts.

- Music educators, like all teachers, need to grow continually in their outlook on their work and their students. They continue to learn until the day they retire from teaching. They also look for and consider new ideas carefully and are not afraid to try different approaches to old problems.

Figure 4.1   Self-Evaluation Form

Self-Evaluation as a Music Teacher

1. What personal characteristics do you possess that you think will help you become a successful music teacher?

2. What personal characteristics do you possess that should be strengthened so that you can become a successful music teacher?

3. What aspects of teaching music are most attractive to you?

4. What aspects of teaching music are least attractive to you?

5. Do you think that you get along well with people—all kinds of people?

6. Do you like children and young people, even when they don't behave the way you would like them to?

7. Are you a fairly well-organized person?

8. Do you like it when other people succeed, or does it bother you when they do?

9. If you could make the same amount of money singing or playing as a performer as you could teaching music, would you rather perform or teach?

- They relate well to other human beings, especially to their students. They empathize with both students and colleagues. They can relate to people from different cultural backgrounds.
- They integrate the subject matter of music with other academic disciplines, especially the other arts. They see music as part of the larger culture.
- They understand their role as teacher. They gain satisfaction, not from receiving personal attention, but rather from seeing growth and success in their students. They realize that they need to lead and inspire their students.
- They are musician-teachers. They realize that they fail to do their job if they don't teach their students musical skills and understandings as well as develop favorable attitudes toward music. They seek out a variety of music for study and performance, and value music for its expressive qualities.

Personal Efficiency

Proper planning requires personal efficiency and organization. Unless teachers have these qualities, both they and their students are apt to find themselves in a state of confusion. Music teachers have been known to forget to order chairs or risers for a performance, lose their own music, fail to keep track of uniforms and instrument numbers (or worse yet, money from ticket sales), and to wait to the last moment to prepare a program for a concert. What rushes of adrenaline these fumblings create! But when confusion reigns, the educational results are reduced. Musicians, along with almost everyone else, may dislike "administrivia." Trivial or not, such details cannot be neglected.

Relations with Professional Colleagues

In some instances, a music program is hampered because of poor relationships between music teachers and the people they work with. For example, if a teacher is personally disagreeable, the school guidance counselors may be less likely to encourage students to enroll in music courses. Some instrumental music teachers compete with choral music teachers, and vice versa. The resulting potential for friction can undermine the total music program and be a waste of emotional energy for the teachers.

Music teachers sometimes overlook the school clerical and custodial staff, or they feel superior to them and let those feelings show. A successful music program depends on the assistance of the nonteaching staff, but thoughtless music teachers occasionally take this help for granted and fail to acknowledge it.

Music teachers should try to take an active interest in school activities. They cannot say on the one hand that music is an integral part of the curriculum and then shy away from serving on school-wide curriculum committees because they feel that music is a special area. Nor should they display little interest in the fate of the football team or drama productions, especially if they want the support of the physical education and theater departments for the music program.

TEACHER AND/OR PERFORMER?

Many undergraduate music majors, maybe including you, are not all that sure about which aspect of music they should be working toward, teaching or performing. And it's seldom an easy or clear choice, especially after you have been in college for only a year or two. The world of professional performing—singing in a musical in New York City, playing trumpet with the Chicago Symphony Orchestra, playing in a first-rate jazz combo in Las Vegas, or similar situations—sounds glamorous and fun. Some of these jobs pay better than beginning teachers' salaries. Further, one does not have to keep a classroom of lively youngsters "on task," to use an educational phrase. It is often said that if you're not good enough to be a performer, you can always teach. Robert Klotman, a former NAfME president, liked to switch the phrase to say, "If you aren't good enough to be a teacher, then you can be a performer."

Is being a performer all that glamorous and satisfying? To begin with, first-rate jobs in the world of performance are very, very difficult to get. In some cases, especially in popular music, it's as much a matter of luck (mostly by being in the right place at the right time) as it is of one's ability. Recently, five hundred violinists from around the world auditioned for positions in the Chicago Symphony Orchestra.

Many performing jobs require traveling—lots of it. That may be enjoyable for a couple of years, but after awhile one begins to think about settling down and perhaps having a family. This is one reason why quite a few performers in prominent symphony orchestras sometimes have left their positions to teach at the college level. In the popular music world, being a performer sometimes means singing or playing many of the same songs again and again and again, which can become rather monotonous.

The heading for this section includes the word "and" because becoming a music teacher does not mean you must give up performing. On the contrary, it is very desirable that music teachers continue to be active musically. Graduation from college should not mean the end of your days as an active musician and performer. The opportunities to perform are abundant in community orchestras, church choirs, community bands, and with local theater groups. While most of the work is voluntary, sometimes a modest stipend is offered. The main point is that you can still be a part-time performer while also being a full-time teacher.

Teaching someone music (or any other subject, for that matter) offers something that being a performer does not—the satisfaction of helping people learn a skill or information that they would not have acquired without your guidance. A teacher can have an impact on their students for the rest of their lives. That's a really impressive fact.

QUESTIONS

1. Think of two good school music teachers you have had, and then think of two who were not so good. What in their personalities and teaching methods made them either successful or unsuccessful?

2. Think of a community that you know well. If there are professional musicians living there, what efforts are made to promote coordinated efforts between them and the school music teachers? What is the relationship between the private music teachers and the school music teachers? Between the music teachers and the music merchants?

3. What are the most important qualities for a successful music teacher?

4. Why should you avoid trying to imitate the actions or personal characteristics of a particular teacher you admire?

5. What are the benefits of making your living as a performer? What are the less desirable aspects of making your living as a performer?

6. What are the benefits of making your living as a music teacher? What are the less desirable aspects of making your living as a music teacher?

REFERENCES

Ausubel, D. P., Novak, J. D., & Hanesian, H. (1978). *Educational psychology* (2nd ed.). New York: Holt, Rinehart & Winston.

Brenton, M. (1970). *What's happened to teacher?* New York: Avon Books.

Preparing to Be a Music Teacher

5

In one sense, you don't need to think about the content of the program you will follow to become a certified a music teacher. The state in which you attend college and your university or college have already decided that for you. However, you will get much more out of your college experiences if you understand the reasons for the various requirements and how courses and requirements contribute to preparing you to be a successful music teacher.

SPECIFIC OR GENERAL PREPARATION?

It would be ideal if you knew now the exact job you will have after graduation. If that were true, faculty and textbook writers could prescribe what you needed to know and be able to do in order to succeed in that particular job. The best that college instructors and authors can do is offer suggestions that work in a majority of school situations.

Although it may not seem necessary to you now, you are wise to take advantage of whatever help is available. Many college students who have had doubts about what they learned in music methods classes have discovered that once they are out in the real world of teaching, the materials studied years before are really helpful.

The fact that no one can know where or what area of music you will teach means that you may study some things in music methods courses you don't think you will need. You may intend to be a high school band director, yet you are learning something about teaching music to elementary school children. Or you may be a singer who never intends to touch an instrument other than a piano. In either case, you may find yourself responsible for a class or two in elementary school general music or leading an ensemble of instruments as they accompany a choral group. Beginning teachers, especially, are also more likely to work in small schools in which versatility is necessary. The more attractive, specialized positions are already held by experienced teachers.

There is another reason for a broad undergraduate training. Suppose that it could be determined just exactly what you needed to know to be a music teacher, and you were given only those courses. That situation would be like buying only the amount of blanket needed to cover yourself at night. You could lie on your back with your hands at your side as your tailored blanket pattern was traced and then cut. Yes, this procedure would save blanket material. But problems would come up when you wanted to change positions as you slept, because you would have no cover for any other position. A narrowly focused teacher-education program provides little "cover" for a different job in music education.

The concept of preparing music teachers for all grades, kindergarten through grade 12, is justified. Many jobs available to music teachers involve teaching at more than one level. Many of them call for teaching in more than one school. Besides, you may be certified for any area in music in your state, not just one type of music teaching.

APPLYING MUSICAL KNOWLEDGE AND SKILLS

Effective music teachers must also be good musicians. Although they may not play an instrument or sing as well as music majors who concentrated on that one aspect of music, they must know music well. Why? A person can't really teach what he or she doesn't know. In addition to knowing music themselves, they must know it so well that they can teach it to someone else.

Several areas are especially important to future music teachers. One is aural skill. The ear training you receive in college is invaluable in teaching music! People who can't hear what is happening in a musical work have little chance of becoming successful music teachers. Although that statement may seem exaggerated, it is not. Music is an aural art, and aural perception and comprehension are essential skills. And this is true not only for directors of ensembles. General music teachers in elementary and middle schools must also be able to hear wrong notes and faulty intonation.

Knowledge of music history and literature is also necessary. Music teachers select music, which involves knowledge of musical works. They then inform students about the world of music. And the inclusion of "world" here is appropriate. In a time of instant communication and jet planes, as well as large immigrations of people to the United States from every part of the world, knowledge of more than the traditional concert and folk music of Western civilization is desirable.

What you learn in applied music instruction is also vital in becoming a successful music teacher. True, you are seldom going to play trumpet or saxophone solos or sing arias for your school classes, but you are going to teach them about phrases, articulations, and expression in music. These attributes require an understanding that largely comes from experiences involving performing phrases, articulations, and expression. Such points often defy verbal explanations.

Learning in Music Education Courses

What should you be learning in a course that introduces you to the field of music education? That seems simple enough: introductory information about music education. But there is more to it than that, because music education—and your future involvement with it—includes understanding a number of different topics like:

- the reasons why teaching music is important;
- the nature of the teaching process;
- the nature of learning in music;
- the qualifications and characteristics of those who teach music; and
- the nature of the profession of music education, including its development and features.

Some of the information you learn in education courses is different from what you usually encounter in college courses. In music theory classes, you acquire skills in listening and learn about the function of various chords. In music history classes you study musical works and the development of music. Much of this type of information was not known to you before you took those courses. That is only partly true of music education courses in which information is occasionally presented that appears to be as novel as "The sun rises in the east."

Why is information that you may already know sometimes included in music education courses? Why doesn't the instructor or author assume your previous knowledge and move on to the new stuff? There are at least four reasons for including information that may not seem new to you.

1. Some students in the course do not know or have not thought about the topic being examined. Not all students start at the same place in terms of what they know. It is better for an instructor's lectures or the coverage in the textbook to be thorough than it is to omit points that some students need.

2. The "I-knew-it-all-along" phenomenon is probably operating on some of the information that you thought you knew. Social psychologists have repeatedly discovered that people often think they already knew something that later became known to them. Humans have a strong tendency to look back at a situation and to believe that its outcome was obvious, commonsense, and something they could have predicted at the time. In fact, contradictory proverbs are readily available to help people declare the accuracy of their hindsight: "Absence makes the heart grow fonder" versus "Out of sight, out of mind" or "Haste makes waste" versus "He who hesitates is lost." As the Danish philosopher-theologian Søren Kierkegaard concluded, "Life is lived forwards, but understood looking backwards."

3. All of us need reminders once in a while or need to have our attention focused on something that we could have figured out for ourselves, *if* we had taken the time to think about it carefully. All of us, if we took the time, "know" that a teacher should maintain eye contact when teaching a class or group and that a variety of activities is more stimulating for students than grinding away for most of a class period or rehearsal on a single topic or activity. Yet, unless reminded, beginning teachers (and some experienced ones, too!) will ignore these and other commonsense facts that they already "know." Part of what a music education course can do is raise one's consciousness about what may seem simple and obvious. So, once in a while it may be helpful to remind present and future teachers that in fact "the sun rises in the east."

4. Usually (but not always), phenomena involving human behavior are partly known. If you observe life systematically and care-

fully, you will learn what social scientists uncover in their research. This should not be surprising, because it would be illogical to have important information about how human beings act remain totally hidden, only to be uncovered by research. Important new information about human behavior rarely comes "out of a clear blue sky." For example, the fact that the use of heavy doses of criticism is not the best way to motivate most people was probably apparent before that fact was confirmed by research studies.

So, what is the value of research on such topics? Research studies are conducted systematically, often under controlled circumstances, and are therefore more precise and verifiable than the impressions of individuals. And every so often, the unexpected happens. Occasionally the results of research studies involving human behavior do not confirm common sense.

Learning in music education courses consists partly of gaining new information and partly of carefully thinking about the process of teaching. It also includes looking at the teaching of music and those who do it in a way that contributes to a better understanding of what teaching music is.

KNOWLEDGE OF TEACHING TECHNIQUES

Good teachers know how to teach essential aspects of a subject. If a band plays a passage in a staccato style, for example, how does the teacher get the idea of staccato over to the players so they can execute it correctly? Without knowing how to do this, a director must resort to commanding, "Now, make those notes short!" This procedure is all right as a beginning, but experienced teachers know that just telling the students to play short notes is not enough. Teachers should have numerous examples, analogies, and explanations ready when teaching. They cannot stop a class, run to their desks, and thumb through a book to look up a technique or a bit of information. Whenever possible, teachers should anticipate the problems that might be encountered in a certain piece. If a work requires staccato playing, they can review various ideas for playing staccato (it's not the same on every instrument) prior to presenting the piece to the ensemble.

When teaching a performing group, teachers should teach their students to do more than execute the printed music symbols and follow the conductor's gestures. Singing and playing can easily become mechanical, so that students make music in a parrot-like fashion without fully understanding what they are doing. Playing and singing are fine, but they are only a part of music education. Students should also be taught something about the style, harmony, form, rhythmic structure, and composers of the more substantial works the group performs.

Pre-Professional Experiences

Observations

Many states and colleges require that future teachers have contacts with schools and students prior to the student-teaching experience. These contacts are called by a variety of names, but "field experiences" is the most commonly used. The purpose of field experiences is to encourage future teachers to think about and be aware of school situations well before the last semester of their undergraduate preparation, when student teaching usually is assigned. In fact, some colleges and states specify contacts with schools beginning in the freshman year, and often observations of disabled and minority students are also stipulated.

Typically, field experiences take place in a variety of school situations so that future teachers gain a perspective of more than one dimension of the music program. Many of them are for only one time in any single school or with any one teacher. Occasionally, a small-project type of teaching is done in conjunction with a music methods class. For example, two or three students develop and teach a short lesson on playing the recorder to a third grade classroom.

The usefulness of pre-student-teaching experiences depends to a great extent on the attitude of the future teachers. If they are approached as just putting in time to fulfill a requirement, then only a limited benefit will be received from them. On the other hand, if future teachers go into school situations and try to analyze the teaching process (*not* the teacher), they will really benefit from these experiences.

What should future teachers attempt to analyze when they observe school music classes? The teaching process as it was described in Chapter 2. (Surprised?) Because these experiences present only a limited time to observe a teacher, and because there is an ethical question about future teachers attempting after one or two classes to guess the motivation of a teacher, the five questions presented in that chapter should be reduced to four for purposes of observations. For each class, the observing students should answer these questions:

- What was the teacher trying to have students learn?
- What methods did the teacher employ to help students learn?
- What appeared to be the musical background and abilities of the students?
- What were the observable results of the instruction?

In addition, student observers will find it useful to notice how the teacher manages some of the routine matters associated with teaching. Such matters include setup of the room, distribution of music, promptness with which the class is started and conducted, assignment of seats for the students, manner in which attendance is taken, and so on. In no sense are such actions as important as the learning that takes place, but they can affect the educational results and are therefore worth observing.

Student Teaching
Student teaching has three basic purposes:

1. It provides future teachers the opportunity to observe and work with an established, successful teacher. A student teacher is an apprentice. This apprenticeship role permits an intensive observation and testing experience that is considered essential in all teacher-education programs. The cooperating teachers (the term often assigned to such teachers) are generally selected because they are considered to be better than average, although sometimes it's a matter of proximity to the university. The cooperating teacher accepts student teachers largely out of a sense of professional commitment, not to make his or her job easier.

2. Student teaching provides a guided induction into teaching. Student teachers can move step-by-step into situations structured by their cooperating teachers. Consequently, student teachers are not just pushed into a class or rehearsal in which they must either sink or swim.

3. Student teaching establishes the fact that the prospective teacher can in fact teach. Future employers want to know, "How did this person do in front of a class?" A good college record and positive character recommendations are fine, but there is no better test of teaching ability than actually teaching in a real-world situation.

It helps if you are clear on what everyone's role is in the student-teaching experience. Your role as student teacher has already been pointed out: an apprentice. You will be a teacher, but yet not fully. You will usually be closer in age to the students than their teacher, and you are expected to act like a teacher, not a student or an intermediary between the class and the teacher. The students know that you are a student teacher whose time with them will be brief. They also suspect that you won't have a lot to say about their final grades or their chair placement in the clarinet section. In a real sense, the position of student teacher is one of guest or temporary resident. You will be working with someone else's classes in a school in which you are not a permanent employee. You will not be in a position to make significant decisions without the approval of the cooperating teacher, to fill out financial requisitions unless the supervising teacher approves them, or to negotiate a different schedule for music classes.

Yet, you will also be a teacher. By that time you will have had much specialized training for what you are doing. You will be expected to show up promptly each day school is in session. You will be allowed some initiative in what is taught, but such undertakings should always be cleared with the cooperating teacher ahead of time.

The role of a cooperating teacher is that of mentor to the student teacher. A mentor is one who guides, offers constructive help, and answers questions. Offering suggestions for improvement is part of that role, as are commendations for work done well. Student teachers need not agree with every suggestion they receive, but the cooperating teachers' thoughts should be given careful consideration and, in most cases, given a try. In addition, cooperating teachers are responsible for a report to the college or university about your teaching. Often they are asked to write a letter of recommendation for your placement file. For all of these reasons, the value of the student-teaching experience depends very much on the cooperating teachers.

College supervisors usually do not have a major role in the student-teaching situation. They are usually limited in the number of times they can visit a student teacher, because they are also teaching other courses. Even if three to five visits are possible, these usually last for only a couple of classes. The college supervisor's role consists largely of making the initial placement and then serving as a coordinator between the college and the cooperating teachers. If important problems arise in a student-teaching situation, then the college supervisor's role becomes vital. Also, if a college supervisor has observed your teaching, he or she can write a letter of recommendation for you that is more credible than letters from other professors because it reports on your teaching of students.

The amount and type of teaching that a student teacher undertakes depends on each cooperating teacher's opinion of the particular needs of the program. Usually the first week or so is spent observing and learning about the situation. Gradually the student teacher is given more responsibility. Often this initial responsibility consists of working with individuals or small groups and doing menial chores such as passing out books, moving chairs, and grading tests. After a while, the student teacher is given entire classes and eventually most of the cooperating teacher's schedule.

For student teachers who demonstrate initiative, optimism, and a willingness to learn, the student-teacher experience will be a rewarding one.

CONTINUED GROWTH AND SELF-EVALUATION

Although it seems like a long way off, you need to realize that continued growth as a teacher after graduation is both desirable and expected. If you graduate from college at the age of twenty-two, you have forty-three years remaining before you reach the age of sixty-five, which is the most common retirement age for school teachers. Forty-three years! That is a very long time even to think about. But it's an even longer time to remain fresh, vital, and interesting. Without continued growth, teachers run the risk of repeating one year's experience forty-three times rather than improving at least a little bit each year. No one should be in a rut for an entire career!

What can teachers do to continue growing professionally? An obvious way, and one required in most states before permanent certification can be obtained and continued, is to continue study at the graduate level during summers or evenings. These requirements are not demanding and often require as little as two courses within a five-year period, only one of which needs to be in the major area. Also, school districts hold workshops and award teachers "units" that can be substituted for college credits, but few of these local workshops are in the area of music because of the small number of music teachers in comparison to other academic areas.

Professional associations, especially NAfME, are an important means of continuing to grow as a teacher. Other means of professional growth include reading professional journals and their reports of research. Teachers should be aware of the results of studies of music teaching and of practices in music education. Research results are reported at NAfME meetings and in its publications. Music teachers should not be satisfied with answering the question, "Does this teaching procedure work?" Instead, they should ask, "Would another procedure work better?" Being satisfied with something just because it happens to work is like being content spending a lifetime hopping about on one leg. Undoubtedly hopping works, but there is a more efficient way to get around—walking.

Self-Improvement

Even after taking advantage of every opportunity and graduating from a strong music education program, beginning teachers should realize that when all said and done, *they must teach themselves to teach.* No course or series of courses, no professor, no book, and no college can impart enough information about the particular school, its students, and its unique nature to train teachers fully. Teachers finally succeed or fail on their own.

Although self-evaluation has the obvious disadvantage of being subjective, it is the only practical means available to most music teachers. For one thing, self-evaluation is a continuous process. It is not something that occurs once or twice a semester; it should go on in one way or another for every class. In addition, it is done with full knowledge of what you are trying to teach and of the total school situation. And finally, it does not involve the psychological risks of being observed and evaluated by others. Only you will know of your successful and less successful efforts.

Evaluations by others are usually of limited usefulness. School administrators seldom know much about music. Visits by school principals to classrooms often elicit comments about things other than the learning of music. Principals sometimes offer general comments such as, "The students seemed to enjoy the class." Even adjudicators at contests, who are competent in music, listen to the performance of a few prepared works with no knowledge of the school situation. School music supervisors can offer the best critiques for teachers. However, their time available for such work is limited, and many school districts do not even have music supervisors.

Teacher Rating Forms

The use of forms by which students evaluate teachers is common at the college level for professors seeking promotion or tenure, but such forms are seldom used in the schools. Even at the college level, rating forms are of limited value. The ratings given are only partly the result of the instructor's actions. For example, instructors of required courses for freshmen and sophomores seldom rate as high as do instructors of junior- and senior-level courses in the students' major area. Rating forms seem to work best with mature students; they are of little value in elementary and middle schools. The other problem with teacher rating forms is that the responses must be only general reactions about a teacher's work. A general statement that one is, or is not, an effective teacher is not very helpful in improving one's teaching.

Playback of Classes

Another specific means of self-evaluation is the use of videos. You can make videos of several classes or rehearsals to analyze later. Videos serve two purposes. First, they allow a more leisurely and thoughtful analysis of what the class accomplished. Second, they enable you to evaluate your own efforts in teaching the class or rehearsal.

When analyzing a video for self-evaluation purposes, do not ask yourself, "Am I a good teacher?" or "Am I a better music teacher than most other music teachers?" Such comparisons or overall self-evaluation questions are not helpful, relevant, or even answerable in any accurate or useful way. Instead, try these questions:

- Were there unnecessary delays and wasted time?
- Were the points on which I instructed the group the ones that most needed attention?
- Did my suggestions to the group actually result in improvements?
- Were my directions clear and decisive?
- Was my conducting clear and decisive?
- Did I repeat certain words and phrases (e.g., "you know," "umm," or "okay?") so frequently that they became annoying?
- Was the pace of my teaching about right?
- Did I tend to focus attention on one section of the group or class, or did I spread my attention evenly?
- Did I seem to be in charge and focused, or did I let a few students distract me?
- Was my warm-up routine something that the students participated in without much thought, or did they learn something useful?
- Were there relaxing breaks in the rehearsal or class routine—a little humor or something done just for the pleasure of it?

- Specifically, what was accomplished in the class?
- Were the students aware of what I was trying to teach them?
- Did I encourage the students to discover and learn some points for themselves, or did I direct every action?

No one has ever achieved the unattainable status of "perfect teacher." Every teacher is human, and therefore none is perfect. Besides, no teacher is equally effective with all students. However, each teacher's unique strengths can give them a distinctive style of teaching. Such individuality is desirable and can be developed along with the requisites of sensitive musicianship and personal maturity. Teachers need to analyze their work throughout their entire careers if they are to achieve their full potential as a teacher.

QUESTIONS

1. Why isn't it useful for music education professors or writers to provide specific cookbook-like directions for teaching music classes or rehearsals?
2. Why do music teachers need to be good musicians?
3. Why should music teachers today know more than the traditional concert and folk music of Western civilization?
4. What examples can you think of that could demonstrate a music teacher's knowledge of teaching techniques?
5. What are the main reasons for requiring future teachers to observe classes and begin participation in teaching before student teaching?
6. In the student-teaching situation, what is the role of student teachers? The cooperating teachers? The college supervisors?
7. Why is it so important for music teachers to continue to grow professionally throughout their entire careers?
8. What are some ways in which music teachers can continue to grow professionally after graduation from college?

PROJECT

Think of three different things that you have learned in music theory class, in music history class, or in applied music lessons in the last three weeks. Then decide how each of those things can help you become an effective music teacher. Share your thinking with other students in your music education class.

The Music Education Profession

Music teachers are never completely alone in their work, even though they may be the only teacher of the subject in a particular school. Their work is affected to some degree by what other music teachers have done in the past and are currently doing. Teachers usually succeed other music teachers in a job, and so they inherit a legacy from their predecessors. If, for example, the previous choral teacher devoted their main efforts to a big musical each year, the students and community may have established the tradition of an annual musical.

Many administrators and music teachers are aware of what goes on in neighboring school districts, and they tend to make comparisons among school music programs. They are sometimes influenced by what similar school districts are doing.

Also, all school music teachers are involved in the same general type of work. The same conditions and public attitudes affect everyone who teaches music in the schools. When a school music program succeeds, music education in general benefits. Unfortunately, every music program that fails hurts music education, at least a little bit.

WHAT IS A PROFESSION?

Music education is often spoken of as a profession, but is it? What characteristics should a type of work possess in order that it earn the distinction of being a "profession"? Four factors are essential.

First, the work of a profession requires extensive education and preparation, usually a baccalaureate degree from college and often a year of additional study. A medical doctor graduates from college and completes three or four years of medical school plus several more years of residency. School music teachers do not have that much training, but they have earned an undergraduate college degree and often have completed at least one year of graduate study.

A second characteristic of a profession is the responsibility for making decisions. An architect plans—makes decisions about—the design and construction of a building. Electricians, plumbers, and many other workers carry out specific tasks according to specific directions. Music teachers not only make decisions about how and what students learn in music classes, they are also responsible for carrying them out.

A third characteristic of a profession is the commitment to the job shared by the membership. Most professionals do not think of their work as only a nine-to-five effort. They work more than the minimum number of hours, and they do so when no one tells them they have to. It's not unusual for them to take work home. Most music teachers are committed to their profession. In fact, their deep sense of commitment sometimes leads to frustration if the public and school administrators don't seem to view a teacher's work as particularly important and don't support it very well.

A fourth characteristic of a profession is that it has an organization that is mainly concerned with the advancement of the profession, not with the welfare of its members. This is the main difference between a union and a professional association. A union's main obligation is to improve the pay and working conditions of its members. A professional organization seeks to keep its members current on developments in the field and to provide for their continued growth in carrying out their work.

The National Association for Music Education

The professional association of school music teachers in the United States is NAfME—National Association for Music Education. Until 1998, its name was Music Educators National Conference. Because the word "conference" implied an event, the more accurate current name was adopted. NAfME consists of the national organization and fifty-three state-federated units. It works to advance music education in a number of ways. One is the in-service education of its members. This continuing education is accomplished through conferences and the publication of books, videos, and journals. The *Music Educators Journal* (now available only online), is its main vehicle of communication of professional ideas, but its list of serial publications includes research and information on other specialized areas. Most state units also publish magazines, many of them online.

A second way NAfME seeks to advance music education is through its efforts to inform others—school administrators and board members, parents, elected officials, and the general public—about the values and nature of music education. These efforts include Music in Our Schools Month, a dedicated website, pamphlets, spot announcements on radio and television, and cooperative efforts with other groups interested in promoting music and music study. These outreach efforts also include contacting governmental leaders and agencies to inform them about the particular needs of music education. Because the health of school music programs depends on the support of others, informing people about music education is a very important part of its work.

A third way the association seeks to advance music education is by serving as the "conscience" of the profession. Although such a role is neither easy nor popular, it is vital if the music education profession is to be effective and respected. Some person or some organization is needed to encourage music teachers to look at themselves and their work in an objective, analytical way to see how it affects students and the image it presents to the general public. It is important that music teachers do the right things, not just do things well.

To the degree that NAfME is successful in promoting music education, all music teachers and students benefit. And much of its success depends on how united music teachers are in supporting it. Smaller specialized groups within music education, such as choral directors and elementary music specialists in one method or another, cannot speak for music education as a whole. Teachers who are attracted to a specialized organization should still retain their commitment to and membership in NAfME. If they don't, the profession risks fragmentation and falling prey to the "wolves" of poor financial and administrative support.

BEING A MEMBER OF A PROFESSION

How do you become a member of the music education profession? Fortunately, you do not have to wait until you have graduated and have a job as a music teacher. In fact, securing a job, as important as that is, is only one step in the process. The first step can be taken now, and it is the most important one: Begin thinking of yourself as a professional music educator. Being a member of a profession is partly a matter of attitude, of the way you think about your work and preparation for that work. That way of thinking is closely related to the characteristics of a profession presented earlier in this chapter. For one, it means securing the education necessary to become a music teacher. But more than that, it means viewing the music and music education courses you take as vital components of your professional preparation.

Being a member of a profession also means thinking about your work as more than a job. A professional person sees his or her work in a larger and more meaningful context. For example, teaching music is not just getting students to sing songs or play an instrument. Rather, it is using singing and playing instruments as a means of teaching music to students, which is something that will enrich their lives now and in the years to come. The difference between those two views of teaching may seem like hairsplitting, but it isn't. It represents the essential difference between just having a job and being a true professional.

People who think like professionals usually do certain things. One is that they join their professional organization, which in the case of music education is NAfME. The association sponsors collegiate groups designed specifically for bringing prospective music teachers into the profession. Collegiate chapters of NAfME are found in more than 600 colleges and universities throughout the United States. The dues are about one-third those asked of teaching members, and yet student members receive all the benefits, including the *Music Educators Journal*.

You should become active now in your student chapter. It offers a variety of activities and presentations that supplement your music methods courses. In addition, the contacts you make and the interest your participation demonstrates to future employers can be beneficial. If your NAfME chapter isn't all that you think it should be, become active in it and make it better.

In addition to joining NAfME, you should begin reading the professional journals in music education. The articles in the *Music Educators Journal* are a good place to begin, but don't stop there. Read the magazines that cover your particular areas of interest—journals such as *The Choral Journal, The Instrumentalist,* and others.

Try to attend a conference of music educators. Although distance and expense may make attendance difficult, find out if such an experience is possible. Registration fees at association conferences and those of its state units are greatly reduced for student members, and expenses can be reduced by sharing rides and rooms. These events, especially the national conferences and those of medium- and large-sized states, are very impressive and professionally stimulating.

A profession consists of people. Music education and NAfME are only nice abstractions unless people breathe life into them. Therefore, the quality of the music instruction students receive depends on the ability of the people who teach them music and their sense of professionalism about their work.

EDUCATING OTHERS ABOUT MUSIC EDUCATION

There is more to being a music teacher than teaching classes, managing supplies, and grading students. In addition to teaching, all music teachers should devote a small amount of time and effort to educating others about the purposes and value of music in the schools. Music educators understand the value of having music in the school curriculum, but most people do not. It's not that they don't want music in the schools. Instead, it's that they don't understand its value for school students. Therefore, when money is short, the support for music is too often "soft." Budget cuts resulting in the loss of teachers and time for music are often the result.

Furthermore, uninformed persons tend to look for the wrong things in forming opinions about the music program in their schools. A win by a band or choir at a contest, even one of little significance, is often misconstrued as meaning that the school system has a really good music program. In addition, almost all the public's opinions are formed from hearing or seeing performing groups. But these groups often involve only 10 or 15 percent of the students in most high schools! As a result, music for the vast majority of the students is largely unnoticed and ignored.

What could music educators do to build better public understanding? Here are several suggestions for doing this:

1. Make public performances into "informances." Instead of just performing music for an audience, informances focus on educating audiences about both the music *and* the educational aspects of learning the particular work. If a group is singing a song, the audience should be informed (preferably by a student, not the teacher) about what they have learned about the music and its social and musical qualities, in addition to just perform-

ing it. The same can be true of playing the autoharp, creating an Orff composition, and other ways in which their performance of the music has enriched their understanding and appreciation of music.

2. Hold a "Parent's Night" in which parents sit in the same section of the band or choral group and sing or follow along in the music with their son or daughter. The evening could include the group sight-reading a work, rehearsing one they have worked on to some extent, and can conclude with one they have learned quite well.

3. Another program could consist of the music that students will perform at an upcoming solo and ensemble competition. The students not only perform their chamber work, they also tell about its musical features.

4. Have one or more students briefly describe the activities that the band or choral group is involved in during the school year.

Professional Musicians

School music programs are affected by the other music activities and interests in the community. A city or town with an active musical life helps the school music program. In turn, effective school music programs contribute to the level of music in communities. For these reasons, music educators should promote music activities in the community. Music teachers should also work to bring professional performers into the schools. To the extent possible, in-school performances by professional performers and educational concerts should be jointly planned ventures between school music teachers and performers. The benefits are greater when such cooperation takes place.

Attempts have been made to define the domains of professional musicians and of school groups. In 1947, MENC, the American Association of School Administrators, and the American Federation of Musicians drew up a comprehensive Music Code of Ethics (see appendix A) that specifies which activities are the domain of school music groups and which should be left to professional musicians. This code has been reaffirmed several times since 1947.

Music Merchants

In addition to maintaining ethical relationships, music teachers need to work with music merchants in an effort to promote music.

Clearly, it is in the interest of both parties to do so. School music events can be publicized in their stores. In many cases, music merchants have instrumental rental programs in which the rental fee for the first semester or year is applied to the purchase of the instrument. When using one of these programs, the school district does not need to own a large inventory of instruments. This arrangement also spares the school district insurance and repair costs.

Contacts between music teachers and music merchants should also be conducted ethically. Because music teachers are usually employed by the public, they should treat everyone equally. They should not accept personal favors or commissions from merchants. The acceptance of gratuities has a way of obligating the teacher and gives the appearance of favoritism. The choice of store and purchases made should be determined solely on the basis of the quality of goods and services in relation to the cost. When purchases amount to $200 or more, it is wise that bids be secured. Competitive bidding encourages the best price from the merchants and provides proof that business transactions are handled fairly and openly.

Private Music Teachers

The level of the school music program can be advanced considerably by the efforts of capable private music teachers. This is especially true in the case of instrumental students who have progressed beyond intermediate levels. Because few school music teachers know advanced techniques on more than one instrument, the progress of the school band or orchestra depends, in part, on the availability of private instruction. The names of private teachers could be listed on concert programs as a means of recognizing their contributions to the success of the ensemble.

Many students, especially at the elementary and middle school levels, take piano lessons. It's a logical area for private instructors and school music teachers to work together. For example, piano students can learn the simple accompaniments to one or two of the songs in the music series materials. Such an experience would give their private study, which is usually individual, a practical application as it offers them recognition for their extra musical activity.

Ethical relationships should also be maintained with private music teachers. Never should the work of an incompetent private teacher be deprecated publicly; that person should simply not be recommended. Whenever possible, music teachers should provide interested parents with the names of more than one competent private teacher. Many communities have professional associations for private instructors, especially for piano. Offering a membership list can be useful in providing recommended teachers.

Should a school music teacher also teach his or her students privately for pay outside of school hours in school facilities? This is a sensitive issue, one that should be discussed with the school principal before it is undertaken. In a few states, it is forbidden by law or school regulation. In any case, the music teacher must be careful about appearing to require private lessons with him or her for a student to earn a higher chair in a section or opportunity to solo with the ensemble.

Community Organizations

Community service clubs and organizations, and especially an area arts council, should not be ignored. Service clubs sometimes provide scholarship help to enable worthy students to study, and on occasion they also help with funding travel by ensembles. Additionally, these groups are a good means of getting information about the music program to the public. The arts council represents a ready-made group that supports the arts, and such support can be valuable if the music program faces financial cutbacks.

Parents

The most useful contacts music teachers have with the public are the parents of the students. Information should be supplied to parents periodically about the activities and goals of the music program. PowerPoint presentations, videos, and brochures can be prepared and used to explain the program. In some instances, parent support groups have been of great help in furthering secondary school performing groups, especially bands. When possible, music teachers should steer the interests of such organizations toward the entire music program, not just one segment of it.

Parents look to music teachers for guidance when their child is contemplating a career in music. School guidance counselors may also be involved in such matters, but their knowledge about music is usually limited. To assist students who are considering music teaching and other music careers, NAfME has prepared materials on careers in music.

TEACHERS AND EDUCATIONAL GOALS

Teachers have both opportunities and limitations in determining the goals in public education. They must accept the broad goals endorsed by society as well as the educational system. Teachers who act contrary to these goals reduce the total effectiveness of the schools, to say nothing of possibly losing their jobs. For instance, teachers cannot teach the violent overthrow of the government or stage performances containing morally questionable scenes without detracting from the results the schools seek to achieve. These broad mandates apply to music teachers just as much as they do to other teachers.

The educational mandates guiding teachers are broad and general. They are something like the directions a passenger gives a taxi driver. The rider gives the destination, but decisions about the best way to get there are the driver's, because he or she is knowledgeable in getting around that city. There are some general restrictions, such as not running into other cars or driving on the sidewalk, which a passenger doesn't need to state specifically. Taxi drivers, like teachers, make the detailed decisions about the best way of reaching the destination and implement them as intelligently and efficiently as possible.

Who finally decides what the specific objectives are for music classes—administrators, boards of education, governmental agencies, or teachers? The forces that affect educational goals and objectives are diverse and often conflicting. States authorize local school boards to oversee education, and school boards then employ administrators to guide the daily efforts of education. But the matter does not stop there. Teachers can also influence decisions within school systems. Because administrators rarely know as much about each subject matter as the teachers who are specialized in their area, they must depend on music teachers for guidance and leadership. Then, after considering the many needs in the school system, they will try to render fair and equitable decisions about how fully the recommendations of the music teachers can be implemented. Unless administrators are informed by the music faculty about what is needed, they will assume that the present situation is satisfactory.

The detailed, within-class decisions are the responsibility of each teacher. There is no way for administrators to oversee such matters. There simply isn't time for them to look over the shoulder of every teacher, and (except for music supervisors) they lack the musical knowledge to make specialized musical decisions. Very few school administrators know the correct embouchure for French horn or the Kodály-Curwen hand signs.

The support of school administrators and school boards is critical to the fate of school music programs. For this reason, educating them about school music programs is a necessary part of every music teacher's work.

QUESTIONS

1. What are the four main characteristics of a profession?
2. What are the differences between a professional association and a union?
3. In what ways does NAfME attempt to advance music education?
4. How can thinking of yourself as a professional music educator influence your outlook toward the music and music education courses you take? Your participation in your student chapter?
5. In what ways can music educators and professional musicians work together?
6. In what ways can private music teachers benefit the school music program?
7. In what ways do music teachers influence the overall goals of the school music program?

PROJECT

Select two articles from the *Music Educators Journal* written in recent years. Report on each article using the following form. One report could be verbal to your class and the other could be written.

Article Report Form

Title of article:

Author:

Magazine or journal:

Date of publication:

Main points of the article:

Subpoints in the article:

Applications of its main points to music education:

Development of
the Profession

Because music has been around since the dawn of civilization, the teaching of music, at least in an informal way, has also been around for a very long time. The first major writings on the value of learning music come from the ancient Greeks around 400 BC. Plato believed in the doctrine of ethos—the idea that music affected moral character. For this reason, he advocated music in the education of every citizen, which in those days was a rather exclusive status. Some movement instruction involved rhythm and was included in physical education, but it would not be recognized as being music in today's terms.

In the early universities of the thirteenth century, music was considered one of the seven liberal arts along with grammar, logic, rhetoric, arithmetic, astronomy, and geometry. It was, therefore, included in the curriculum of the universities being founded in Italy, France, and England. The fascination with music was not with its artistic or tonal properties, but rather with its acoustical ratios and other mathematical attributes. These were thought to hold certain secrets of the cosmos. The study of music consisted of thinking and talking about music, not performing it.

A more practical type of music education was found in conservatories, which were founded in the 1500s. The word "conservatory" comes from an Italian word for "orphanage." In fact, early conservatories were also orphanages. One of the most famous conservatories was the Ospedale della Pietà in Venice, where Antonio Vivaldi taught and composed many works of music for the teenage girls to perform. One can only guess why orphans were selected to be trained as performers.

Perhaps it was believed that because they had no families, a life "on the road" (typical of musicians in those days) would not bother them.

Music was undoubtedly taught on an individual, one-to-one basis, especially to women of the upper classes and to boys who planned to make their livelihoods as musicians. But music education in schools and colleges as we know it today is a relatively recent development.

BEFORE 1800

European music came to America with the first settlers to Virginia and Massachusetts, but it is not clear when professional instruction in music began. The first music instruction books were the product of John Tufts, a minister, who in the early eighteenth century wanted to teach the churchgoing colonists to sing psalms and hymns. He devised a tetrachord system of notation in which the octave is broken into two identical halves. Tufts chose the tetrachords E F G A and B C D E, which he identified by the syllables *mi, fa, so,* and *la* (Lowens, 1964). His system was later adapted into "shape notes" in which each of the four shapes of the note heads indicates a syllable. Shape notes are still seen occasionally in the notation of some hymnals, especially in the southern states.

Tufts' efforts were followed by the "singing school" movement in which music teachers traveled from one town to another to give lessons for a few weeks. The singing schools existed primarily to teach church music.

THE NINETEENTH CENTURY

A Swiss educator, Johann Heinrich Pestalozzi, had a major influence on education in the first half of the nineteenth century. Although he was not a music teacher himself, his ideas were adapted by others for teaching music. One adaptation was by George Nageli, who wrote a book in 1810 entitled *The Theory of Instruction in Singing According to Pestalozzian Principles (Die Gesangbildumstehre nach Pestalozzischen Grundsatzen).* Another early proponent of Pestalozzian ideas was Joseph H. Naef, who had been a member of Pestalozzi's staff in Europe before immigrating to America in 1806. In 1809, he founded an elementary school and in 1830 presented his ideas on music teaching according to the principles of Pestalozzi:

1. To teach sounds before signs—to make the child learn to sing before he learns the written notes or their names;

2. To lead him to observe by hearing and imitating sounds, their resemblances and differences, their agreeable and disagreeable effects, instead of explaining these things to him—in short, to make active instead of passive in learning;

3. To teach but one thing at a time—rhythm, melody, and expression are to be taught and practiced separately, before the child is called to the difficult task of attending to all at once;

4. In making the students practice each step of these divisions, until they master it, before passing to the next;

5. In giving the principles and theory after the practice, and as induction from it;

6. To analyze and practice the elements of articulate sounds in order to apply them to music;

7. To have the names of the notes correspond to those used in instrumental music. (Birge, 1966, pp. 38–39)

Lowell Mason is generally considered to be the father of music in American schools. He was a man of enormous versatility and vision who became convinced that instruction in music was good for all children. In 1836, he petitioned the school board in Boston for the inclusion of vocal music in the elementary schools. A special committee of the board was appointed to consider the proposal. In 1837, it submitted a report containing a positive recommendation. The report is interesting not only for its quaint syntax but also for the reasons it provides to justify the introduction of music in the Boston schools:

Let music be examined by the following standards:

1. Intellectually. Music had its place among the seven liberal arts, which scholastic ages regarded as pertaining to humanity. Arithmetic, Geometry, Astronomy, and Music—these formed the quadrivium. Memory, comparison, attention, intellectual faculties—all of them are quickened by a study of its principles. It may be made to some extent a mental discipline.

2. Morally. It is unphilosophical to say that exercises in vocal music may not be so directed and arranged as to produce those habits of feeling of which these sounds are the type. Happiness, contentment, cheerfulness, tranquility—these are the natural effects of music.

3. Physically. It appears self evident that exercises in vocal music, when not carried to an unreasonable excess, must expand the chest and thereby strengthen the lungs and vital organs. Judg-

ing then by this triple standard, intellectually, morally, and physically, vocal music seems to have a natural place in every system of instruction which aspires, as should every system, to develop man's whole nature. (Birge, 1966, p. 41)

Later, it continues:

What is the great object of our system of popular instruction? Are our schools mere houses of correction, in which animal nature is to be kept in subjection by the law of brute force and the stated drudgery of distasteful tasks? Not so. They have a nobler office. They are valuable mainly as a preparation and a training of the young spirit for usefulness and happiness in coming life. Now, the defect of our present system, admirable as that system is, is this, that it aims to develop the intellectual part of man's nature solely when, for all the true purposes of life, it is of more importance, a hundredfold, to feel rightly than to think profoundly. Besides, human life must and ought to have its amusements. Through vocal music you set in motion a mighty power which silently, but surely, in the end, will humanize, refine and elevate a whole community.

From this place first went out the great principle, that the property of all should be taxed for the education of all. From this place, also, may the example, in this country, first go forth of that education rendered more complete by the introduction by public authority, of vocal music into our system of popular instruction. (Birge, 1966, p. 47)

THE TWENTIETH CENTURY

It is difficult for us who live in the early years of the twenty-first century to imagine what life and schools were like in 1900. Americans lived mainly on farms and in small towns. The automobile and telephone were just beginning to appear; radio was a couple of decades in the future, and television was still four decades away. A woman's place was generally understood to be in the home, and most men were employed at jobs that required physical labor—farming, mining, and so on. Having enough food to eat and a place to live was a major concern in life because neither could be assumed. There was no social security system or unemployment or medical insurance. Life expectancy was much shorter.

Education was different, too. Most young people did not attend school beyond eighth grade. They often went to small, one-room schools in which rote learning prevailed. Most teachers were single women, and they sometimes had less than a year of training beyond high school at a teacher training institution. Few teenagers went to high school, which offered mainly a college preparatory program consisting of subjects such as Latin, algebra, and history. There were no football games or other extracurricular activities or subjects such as home economics and typing. Music education was almost entirely vocal music. In many schools, it consisted of a little singing by rote; in other schools, it included drills on sight-singing.

Changes of enormous importance were on the horizon in 1900, however. Not only would America begin to nearly triple in size, but it would also change from a rural to an urban nation. Society was to become far more complex, and the roles of women and minorities were to change greatly. Schools were changing, too. For example, from 10 percent of the potential number of students attending high school in 1900, the percentage increased to over 70 percent by 1940 (Department of Health, Education, and Welfare, 1970). By the end of the century, that figure reached 95 percent. Along with this change came a much richer and more varied curriculum, one that included both instrumental and choral music. Surprising as it may seem today, the first instrumental groups in schools were orchestras, not bands. In places like Richmond, Indiana, and Winfield, Kansas, enterprising teachers such as Will Earhart and Edgar B. Gordon were developing fine instrumental music programs.

After World War I

Following their service in the war, a number of military band directors began teaching in schools, which led to an interest in bands. Several group instrumental methods were published, and high-quality music programs were beginning in major cities such as Cleveland, Los Angeles, Chicago, Detroit, Cincinnati, Kansas City, and others.

The growth of music, especially instrumental music, was rapid in the 1920s and 1930s, and only a limited number of teachers trained to teach at the high school level were available. This movement of professional musicians into teaching was accelerated by the introduction of "talking pictures" in 1927 (resulting in the loss of pit orchestra jobs in theaters) and by the Great Depression that began in 1929 (resulting in general unemployment). These conditions had a profound effect on the type of instruction offered.

The 1920s also saw the beginning of the progressive education movement. Based on the ideas of philosopher-educator John Dewey, the movement emphasized the learning process rather than subject matter content and the need for a correlation between the students' school and life experiences. Two results of such thinking were an emphasis on the involvement of the classroom teacher in the teaching of music and the correlation of music with other school subjects, especially social studies.

At the same time, however, conflict existed in music education over the importance of sight-singing. A sizable number of music educators advocated drill and practice in reading music so students would gain enough skill in reading music to participate in music throughout the rest of their lives. Other music educators saw music largely as enrichment of children's lives and a handmaiden to other subjects. As with so many disputes, this one was never settled.

After World War II

The 1940s were consumed first with the conduct of World War II and then later with the recovery from that conflict. The decades of the 1950s and 1960s were good ones for education in a number of ways. The number of children in school represented a high watermark in terms of the percentage of the total population, reaching a level that may never be equaled again. This situation meant there were many families who were involved with and supportive of the schools. In addition, there was much faith in education as a means of improving society and life. Music programs enjoyed unprecedented growth during these decades.

The 1960s

This decade is especially interesting because of the number and size of the national programs that were initiated. A wave of concern over the quality of schools filled newspapers and popular magazines. Much of the same language heard in the cries for school reform in the late 1960s were heard again in the 1980s and again in the early years of the twenty-first century. In the 1960s, the responses to the calls for reform were a number of major grants from the federal government. In other cases, professional organizations, including NAfME, also sponsored large national events and projects.

The best known of these national events for music educators was the Tanglewood Symposium, which was held at Tanglewood, Massachusetts, for two weeks during the summer of 1967. Sponsored by the

Presser Foundation and NAfME, its theme was "Music in a Democratic Society." Its participants included leaders from business, education, labor, government, and the arts, as well as music educators. The many papers read and the conclusions to the discussion held during the symposium were published in a documentary report. The final declaration of the symposium was:

> Music Educators at Tanglewood agree that:
> - Music serves best when its integrity as an art is maintained.
> - Music of all periods, styles, forms, and cultures belongs in the curriculum. The musical repertory should be expanded to involve music of our time in its rich variety, including currently popular teenage music and avant-garde music, American folk music, and the music of other cultures.
> - Schools and colleges should provide adequate time for music programs ranging from preschool through adult or continuing education.
> - Instruction in the arts should be a general and important part of education in the senior high school.
> - Developments in educational technology, educational television, programmed instruction, and computer-assisted instruction should be applied to music study and research.
> - Greater emphasis should be placed on helping the individual student to fulfill his needs, goals, and potentials.
> - The music education profession must contribute its skills, proficiencies, and insights toward assisting in the solution of urgent social problems as in the "inner city" or other areas with culturally deprived individuals.
> - Programs of teacher education must be expanded and improved to provide music teachers who are specially equipped to teach high school courses in the history and literature of music, courses in the humanities and related arts, as well as teachers equipped to work with the very young, with adults, with the disadvantaged, and with the emotionally disturbed. (Choate, 1968, p. 139)

The effects of the symposium were felt in music education long after the event itself was over. It provided direction for a number of NAfME efforts, as well as topics for special issues of the *Music Educators Journal*.

The Juilliard Repertory Project began in 1964 and was supported by a large grant from the U.S. Office of Education to the Juilliard School of Music. Its purpose was to develop a body of authentic and meaningful music to enrich the repertoire of music available to music teachers in the elementary schools. The music, compiled by musicologists, music education leaders, and school music teachers, was divided into seven categories based on historical style periods, plus folk music. The selection process was for the musicologists to select material and then submit the works to a panel of leaders in music education, who decided which works would be field-tested in the schools.

Four hundred pieces of music were tested, with 230 vocal and instrumental works retained for the Juilliard Repertory Library. This collection was published by Canyon Press of Cincinnati. Because of the amount of material (384 pages), the collection was also published in eight volumes of vocal music and four of instrumental music.

Two projects of the 1960s promoted creativity and new music. The most important of these was the Young Composers Project, begun in 1957 with a grant from the Ford Foundation. The idea was to place ten young (under the age of 35) composers as composers-in-residence in school systems with strong music programs. The hope was that the young composer would learn about the opportunities and challenges of writing for school groups and promote his or her interest in contemporary music in the school and community. By 1962, thirty-one composers had been placed in school systems. In many ways, the response to the program was good, but the composers reported that many music teachers were poorly prepared to deal with contemporary idioms. Therefore, in 1962, the project was increased to become one of the Ford Foundation's ten major programs. NAfME submitted a proposal to the foundation for what was to become the Contemporary Music Project (CMP). The program ended in 1973.

The purposes of the project were to:

- increase the emphasis on the creative aspect of music in the public schools;
- create a solid foundation or environment in the music education profession for the acceptance, through understanding, of the contemporary music idiom;
- reduce the compartmentalization that now exists between the profession of music composition and music education for the benefit of composers and music educators alike;
- cultivate taste and discrimination on the part of music educators and students regarding the quality of contemporary music used in schools; and
- discover, when possible, creative talent among students. ("Contemporary Music Project," 1973)

During its final ten years, the CMP devoted much of its attention to the skills and knowledge required to deal with all types of music, although the placing of composers in schools continued. Its process-centered approach included three components: performing, organizing, and describing. This manner of teaching was often referred to as the "common elements approach." Through this approach, the CMP maintained, the compartmentalization in the music profession could be greatly reduced.

Two major pieces of legislation were enacted in 1965: the Elementary and Secondary Education Act and the National Foundation on the Arts and Humanities. The Elementary and Secondary Education Act provided massive funding ($1.3 billion in 1965) in five sections called "titles." Title I provided grants to schools for the education of disadvantaged children. The nature of the services supported with these funds was left up to the local school, and music instruction or activity could be included under this title.

Because most of the funds were provided under Title I, it had the most impact. Some school districts hired music teachers and purchased music books and equipment for use in areas with large numbers of low-income families. It was estimated that about one-third of the 8.3 million children receiving the benefits of Title I were involved with music or art (Lehman, 1968).

Legislation establishing the National Endowment for the Arts and the National Foundation for the Humanities was also enacted in 1965 "to help create and sustain not only a climate encouraging freedom of thought, imagination, and inquiry, but also the material conditions facilitating the release of this creative talent" (National Endowment for the Arts, 1975). The National Endowment for the Arts and the National Endowment for the Humanities were both created under this legislative action. During its first years, the NEA's education efforts consisted mainly of its Artists-in-Schools program in which professional performers and artists provided performances or special instruction on a visiting basis.

The 1970s

The decade started out well for education, but some long-term trends were soon to have their negative impact. For one, the national programs of the 1960s failed to have anywhere near the impact their supporters hoped for. Many of the curriculum projects developed materials that were too difficult or did not relate well to the students and teachers for whom they were intended. The result was sometimes disenchantment with such efforts.

Then, the percentage of the population with children in school decreased following the "baby boom" of the 1950s and 1960s and the number of teachers exceeded demand. The result was the "riffing" (reduction in force) of many teachers and the hiring of fewer beginning teachers. In addition, the competition for tax dollars became more intense with the demands for health care, benefits for the elderly, law enforcement and prisons, and special education.

The decade was not without some attention to education at the national level. The Education for All Handicapped Children Act enacted in 1975 mandated special education for students with disabilities. Although some states were providing programs for these students, it was estimated that prior to this legislation, only half of the eight million children with disabilities received any kind of arts education (Graham, 1975).

The law had two effects for music teachers. One was to require some of them to become competent in teaching music to children with special needs—those who are emotionally disturbed or physically or mentally challenged. The second result was the mainstreaming of students with disabilities into music classes. The regulations of the law require that "to the maximum extent appropriate, children with disabilities are educated with children who are not disabled" and that "special classes, separate schooling, or other removal of children with disabilities from the regular educational environment occurs only when the nature or severity of the disability is such that education in regular classes with the use of supplementary aids and services cannot be achieved satisfactorily" (*Federal Register*, 2006).

NAfME has long maintained that music teachers should he involved in placement decisions for students with disabilities in music classes (Mark, 1986). This suggestion has often been ignored by school principals, with the result that in some cases mainstreaming students has caused serious problems in educating the other students in a class.

The 1980s

A combination of circumstances led to renewed national concern in the 1980s about the quality of education in American schools. One was America's decreasing ability to compete economically with Japan and Germany—two of the countries it had defeated a generation earlier in World War II. A better-educated workforce was perceived as a serious need. Another circumstance was the decline of scores by high school juniors and seniors on the Scholastic Aptitude Test (SAT) in comparison with several European countries. Despite the fact that many more American students were taking such tests, these scores were viewed as evidence of a general decline in the quality of their education. Another concern was the deterioration of the school systems in many large cities. Crime, drugs, and absenteeism had replaced learning in too many places.

The solution in the 1980s to such educational problems was not through large-scale, federally funded programs, as was true in the 1960s. Instead, it was in highly publicized reports that required only a small expenditure of funds compared to new educational programs. The federal government sponsored some of these efforts and private foundations undertook sponsorship of others. The best known was a product of the National Commission on Excellence in Education. The commission, appointed by President Reagan and made up of business people and educators, issued a report in 1983 entitled *A Nation at Risk: The Imperative for Educational Reform*. Its ringing phrases claimed many weaknesses in American education—diluted curricula, limited class time, not-very-able teachers, insufficient requirements, and a general lack of academic rigor. The report suggested more demanding graduation requirements: four years of English, three years of mathematics, three years of science, three years of social studies, and one-half year of computer science. College-bound students were also urged to take two years of a foreign language. Unfortunately, *A Nation at Risk* mentioned the arts only twice.

The response to the challenges of *A Nation at Risk* and other national reports was left largely to the states. As with the federal government, rhetoric was much greater than meaningful action at the state level. The most common response was to increase the number of courses required for high school graduation. Generally, these requirements reduced the number of electives, which in turn reduced enrollments in music. Other actions, including lengthening the school year, increasing teacher-certification requirements, and the testing of students and teachers were instituted.

The 1990s

The most significant national effort affecting music and the arts in the 1990s was the publication *National Standards for Arts Education: What Every Young American Should Know and Be Able to do in the Arts*

(1994). It was the product of a national educational effort funded by the federal government called "America 2000" when initiated by President George H. W. Bush in 1989. His idea was to work with the fifty state governors to develop "world class" standards for America's schools. The effort continued with only slight changes after President Clinton, one of the co-chairs of the governors' task force, was elected. The name was changed, however, to "Goals 2000."

The National Standards were important because they carried the imprimatur of the federal government. They were not just the result of one committee's views speaking for only one segment of the profession. Instead, they were a national consensus resulting from a systematic effort on the part of each academic area. In fact, they represented the first effort ever on the part of the federal government to specify subject matter goals in the arts.

Seven curricular areas were designated; the fine arts—not just music—was one of them. Each art was developed by committees from the four fine arts areas: dance, music, theater, and visual arts. Although developed separately by committees composed of educators from each of those areas, the product of each committee's work was required by the Department of Education to be in the same format and style and published in a single document. The final version of the fine arts standards was adopted by Congress and signed by President Clinton in March 1994.

Because states are responsible for education in the United States, the National Standards could only be a recommendation for "best practice." States could either adopt the National Standards as published, or they could adapt them, which is what many states did.

THE TWENTY-FIRST CENTURY

The first major symposium in the twenty-first century was Vision 2020: The Housewright Symposium, which was held in the fall of 1999 at Florida State University and sponsored by NAfME. Speakers and participants devoted their attention to what actions the music education profession should take in the next twenty years. Its concluding declaration contained some of the ideas found in the Tanglewood Declaration.

The most significant action affecting education thus far in this century is the "No Child Left Behind" (NCLB) Act passed by Congress and signed by President George W. Bush in 2001. The purpose of the law was to bring virtually all students up to standard in reading and math by the year 2014 and to combat what President Bush termed "the soft bigotry of low expectations" in which less is expected of some students, especially minority children.

NCLB's effect on music education has not been good because of the emphasis it placed on reading and math. It is only human nature for teachers and administrators to devote attention to the parts of the curriculum that are made publicly visible, which is what happened as a result of the effect of the test scores of individual schools. The amount of time devoted to those two subjects has increased while the attention to other subjects has decreased. The time for music in elementary schools was already below the minimum recommended by NAfME (1994). In many cases, it has been reduced further, and some music teachers have been required to include teaching reading as a part of their responsibilities.

NCLB does have a beneficial effect of placing an emphasis on the assessment of what students learn. All teachers, including music teachers, are asked to gather evidence regarding the results of their teaching.

The 2014 Standards

The other significant project has been the revision in 2014 of the 1994 standards. They are quite different from the standards of twenty years earlier. Instead of one book containing four distinct sections (dance, music, theater, and visual arts) the four areas were homogenized into one process-orientated online document based on three artistic processes: creating, performing, and responding. This change has distinct advantages for the arts, but also limitations in that many terms understandable to musicians had to be avoided and terms more familiar to the other areas used. The 2014 standards are more complicated than the 1994 standards. They require a steeper learning curve if one is to use them to develop a curriculum based on the more recent standards.

You will probably be encountering the 2014 standards again in future methods courses. At that time you will have the chance to work with them and to acquire greater competence in making use of them.

CONCLUSION

Since 1837, when Lowell Mason taught the first music classes in the public schools of Boston, music education has been through a lot.

It has survived wars, depressions, reductions in force, various mandated requirements for schools, and often being near the end of the line when funds are allocated. But today, in spite of all these vicissitudes, virtually every school and school system in the United States has music instruction. That instruction may not be all that music educators know it can and should be, but at least it's there. It has not only survived; in many cases it has thrived. Why? The answer to that question goes back to the ideas presented in Chapter 1. Music and instruction in music are so right and valid that they have endured and will continue to do so in schools in one form or another. If that were not so, music in schools would have long ago faded into oblivion.

QUESTIONS

1. Prior to the late 1950s, what reasons were given for including music in schools?

2. What major changes occurred in high school education between 1900 and 1940?

3. What were the main points of the Tanglewood declaration?

4. What major federal program was passed in 1965 that greatly affected education and the arts?

5. Under what conditions do federal regulations require that students with disabilities be placed in regular classes?

6. In the 1980s, what actions did state and the federal government take with regard to perceived weaknesses in education?

7. What has been the impact of the "No Child Left Behind" Act?

REFERENCES

Birge, E. B. (1966). *History of public school music in the United States.* Reston, VA: Music Educators National Conference.

Choate, R. A. (Ed.). (1968). *Documentary report of the Tanglewood symposium.* Reston, VA: Music Educators National Conference.

College Entrance Examination Board. (1983). *Academic preparation for college: What students need to know and be able to do.* New York: Carnegie Foundation.

Contemporary music project. (1973). *Music Educators Journal, 59*(9), 34.

Department of Health, Education, and Welfare. (1970). *Digest of educational statistics.* Washington, DC: U.S. Government Printing Office.

Federal Register. (2006). "Part II: Department of Education. Assistance to states for the education of children with disabilities and preschool grants for children with disabilities; final rule." Accessed from https://www.gpo.gov/fdsys/pkg/FR-2006-08-14/pdf/06-6656.pdf

Graham, R. M. (1975). *Music for the exceptional child*. Reston, VA: Music Educators National Conference.

Lehman, P. H. (1968). Federal program in support of music, *Music Educators Journal, 55*(1), 53.

Lowens, I. (1964). The first American music textbook. In *Music and musicians in early America*. New York: Norton.

Madsen, C. K. (Ed.). (2000). *Vision 2020: The Housewright Symposium on the future of music education*. Reston, VA: Music Educators National Conference.

Mark, M. L. (1986). *Contemporary music education* (2nd ed.). New York: Schirmer Books.

Music Educators National Conference (MENC). (1994). *Opportunity-to-learn standards for music instruction: Grades pre-K–12*. Reston, VA: Author.

National Association for Music Education (NAfME). (1994). *National standards for arts education: What every young American should know and be able to do in the arts*. New York: Rowman & Littlefield.

National Commission on Excellence in Education. (1983). *A nation at risk: the imperative for educational reform*. Washington, DC: U.S. Department of Education.

National Endowment for the Arts. (1975). *Guide to programs*. Washington, DC: Author.

Content of Music Classes and Rehearsals

Vito Marconi has his middle school band play several B-flat con-cert scales, each in a different rhythm pattern. Next, he has the band play through two other pieces from the music in their fold-ers. Nothing from the warm-up exercises is mentioned again in the rehearsal.

Sharonda Billups has her middle school general music class fig-ure out the words spelled by patterns of notes in the treble and bass clefs. The students study the notes on the sheets she has given them. Then they write the letters for a word like "cabbage" below the notes when they see those notes in the notation.

What did the students in Vito's and in Sharonda's classes learn? What do students learn from playing scales or only naming notes? What did Vito's students learn from the warm-up scales that did not relate to the music played in the rehearsal?

Such questions go to the heart of music teaching, because learning in music classes is the purpose of music education. Just gathering stu-dents together in a class and calling it "music" does not ensure that much learning of music will take place. Music teachers, therefore, should think carefully about what they try to teach. They need to be sure that it's both musically significant and meaningful to the students.

That sounds simple enough. Unfortunately, it isn't. Part of the value of the content of a music class is determined by what precedes and follows it. Naming notes in Sharonda Billups' class could be useful if it is associated with musical sounds. Otherwise, the activity is not of much more value than working crossword puzzles with music symbols and words. Playing scales in Vito Marconi's rehearsal and running through works in the folders is only partly effective, depending on how well he taught the activity and whether the scales are encountered in the music the group is rehearsing.

LEARNING IN MUSIC

The chorus at Wellstone Middle School is singing the Shaker song "Simple Gifts." Students should gain knowledge in at least five areas from singing this attractive song:

1. The syntax of musical sounds
2. The song as a work of music
3. Understandings about musical processes and organization
4. The skills needed in performing and listening to music
5. Attitudes about a particular piece and music in general

Each of these outcomes of learning merits further exploration.

Musical Syntax

If music is organized sound, then a sense of the patterns of sounds is absolutely required for people to recognize those sounds as being organized. Otherwise, the sounds are just a random sonic jumble, something like a cat walking on the keys of a piano.

The analogy between language and music is not a perfect one, but in a number of ways they are much alike. When learning language, children find out that "runs big slowly dog black the" is not an easily understandable pattern. They need similar learning in music, except with musical sounds, of course. A sense of patterns or syntax in language, as well as in music, is developed through experience with speaking and listening. Children enter school with several years' experience in hearing and speaking words. Only after they have had much practice and experience with spoken language are they given the visual symbols for the words they already know aurally.

There is another similarity between language and music. The learning of syntax and the pronunciation of words develop early in life. By the time a child is ten years old, the ability for such learning then begins to decrease. For this reason, it is crucial that children in kindergarten and the primary grades of elementary school be given many opportunities for gaining a sense of musical syntax to be accurate in singing pitches.

The syntax of music is probably the first type of learning that students should acquire in music, because without it the other four areas of learning will not mean much. A strong sense of syntax can carry a person quite a distance in the world of music. For example, most of the early jazz musicians had little formal training and couldn't read music, yet their wonderful intuitive sense for musical patterns more than compensated for their other limitations. They were, however, limited in to a specific type of music.

Musical Works

The vast amount of music created throughout the world over the past couple of thousand years is beyond comprehension. Not only is there concert music ranging from the 3,800 works by Telemann to the 1,600 trouvère and troubadour melodies to Haydn's 104 symphonies, there are also thousands and thousands of pieces of folk music and popular songs. No one, not even the most avid music listener, could possibly listen to each work even once in an entire lifetime. And the amount of music increases each day.

One thing students should learn in music classes is where a particular piece of music belongs in the world of music. In the case of "Simple Gifts," singers should acquire some understanding of the text, melodic characteristics, social setting, and similar information about this work, as well as other types of American folk music. It is not enough just to sing songs in music classes.

One difficult problem for teachers is the selection of music. With limited time for music instruction in elementary schools, teachers can just skim the surface of available music. Again, some hard decisions must be made, and many fine works of music and songs simply cannot be included.

Intellectual Understandings

The intellectual understandings of music involve the formation of concepts about music, the manner of thinking about music, and some knowledge of the process of creating music. Of the three, concept formation is probably the most important for the majority of the students.

Concepts

The dictionary definition of the word "concept" is useful in understanding what concepts are and how they are formed: "an abstract or generic idea generalized from particular instances." Some concepts such as "music" are broad in scope, while others like "tempo" are more specific. The structuring of concepts according to differing degrees of comprehensiveness is similar to the system of classification used in biology—phylum, genus, species, and so on. In music there are conceptual ideas about melody, harmony, form, rhythm, and the like. Subconcepts of melody include ideas about contour, motive, theme, expression, and so on. And each of these subconcepts can be divided further into even more specific categories.

A concept is not the same as its verbal symbol or definition. In fact, a concept can exist without a verbal symbol. A definition is merely the assignment of a verbal "label" to something already formed in the mind. It is more accurate, for example, to think of the generalized quality of dogs as the concept rather than the more specific word "poodle."

People form concepts as they notice similarities and differences among objects and, in the process, organize and classify them. For example, they form a concept of dogs as animals with four legs, one tail, an ability to bark, and an acute sense of smell but are unable to climb trees or see well in the dark. Without previous experience with animals, definitions ("A dog is . . .") and factual statements ("Dogs can bark . . .") are rather meaningless. A concept must first exist on which to affix the verbal symbol. This means that teachers are limited to establishing situations in which the students can form the desired concepts. The generalizing process essential for concept formation must happen in each student's mind. As with a sense of musical syntax, concepts are refined with each experience.

The reason that teachers should be interested in concept formation is that concepts help people think. The fact that words are mental tools as well as a means of communication was established many years ago (Oléron, 1977). Students who have no concept of melody are seriously impaired in their ability to think about, understand, and appreciate melodies. Furthermore, because concepts are generalized ideas, they are far more versatile and flexible than specific ideas. The concept of melody can be applied in all kinds of pieces of music, but the melody to "Simple Gifts" is specific to only that one piece of music. A third virtue of conceptual learning is that basic, general ideas are remembered much better and longer than specific facts.

Way of Thinking

Every field of study—science, history, music—has its mode of thinking, its way of looking at things. A physicist, for example, is interested in the physical properties of sounds; a social scientist is interested in the effect of music on human behavior; a musician is interested in how sounds are manipulated and the tonal effects and compositions that can be created with them. Students should learn to think a bit like scientists in science classes, like social scientists in social science classes, and like musicians in music classes. The appropriate manner of thinking and mental approach is as much a part of the subject as is the factual information associated with it.

How does musician-like thinking differ from other thinking? If you question the proverbial man-on-the-street about his views on music, chances are that you will find that he thinks of music as something for accompanying other activities, such as whistling songs while painting a fence or what he hears on the car radio while driving to work. Almost never will he talk about music as an object for careful consideration by itself. On the other hand, musicians value organized sounds. They think the way Mozart put sounds together in the fourth movement of his Symphony No. 41 is really impressive. In fact, they don't want distractions like painting a fence when they listen to the *Jupiter* symphony. Also, musicians analyze the sounds they listen to. They are interested in figuring out what Mozart did with those sounds. Because they value sounds and analyze them, musicians enjoy concert music more and know more about it than do non-musicians.

Creative Process

Learning in music should not be confined to the re-creation of what others have done. At a level consistent with their musical development, students should engage in creating music through composition and/or improvisation. Such activities are valuable because they:

- require students to think about how sounds are manipulated, which is a central feature of the way musicians think;
- educate students about the process of creating music, including its mental trial and error and sometimes the hard work; and
- allow students to explore their own musical potential and, in that sense, to know themselves better

As valuable as creative activities are for students in learning music, they are only a part of the subject. Students should not be confined to only those works they themselves create, any more than they should be limited to works that someone else has created.

Skills and Activities

The words "skills" and "activities" are not synonymous. Skills refer to physical activities such as vibrato when playing the violin, tonguing passages on the clarinet, and singing a melody at sight. Some music classes make the acquisition of skills a major part of their content. That fact is also true of instrumental music classes and of private instruction in singing or playing an instrument. Other classes usually include some learning of skills.

Activities are actions that students engage in as a means of learning. Students who sing a song are more likely to understand and appreciate it than those who just listen to it, especially if they have not had much experience in music. For example, when English teachers want their students to understand a drama, they have them read sections from a play and discuss the purpose, literature, and technical production. To increase their understanding of certain points, the teacher may have students act out portions of the play in the classroom. This activity furthers their learning about drama, just as activities in music can aid learning it.

Activities, however, cannot substitute for subject matter content. Singing one song after another, class after class, does not contribute much to students' understanding of music or their aesthetic sensitivity. This was the flaw in Vito Marconi's teaching described at the beginning of this chapter. At one time, music programs in the elementary schools were described entirely in terms of activities: singing, playing instruments, creating, rhythmic movement, reading, and listening. But these were activities, not subject matter content. It would have been more accurate to say what students learned through the activity of singing or listening. The goal of music education should not be just to do something in music. Rather, it is to educate students in music, as well as to further that education through the use of appropriate activities.

The division of the subject matter content of music into activities and outcomes, or any other system of categorizing the topic, is somewhat artificial. A musical experience is a complex, unified experience in which most of the categories are involved at the same time. When students sing or play pieces of music, they are usually strengthening their concept about music, gaining some information about it, improving their skill at performing it, and affecting how they feel about the piece in particular and music in general. The extent to which each of these results is achieved depends partly on what the teacher emphasizes. Sometimes music teachers concentrate so much on one category of outcomes that little is accomplished in other categories.

Effective music instruction avoids this pitfall; instead, it strikes a reasonable balance among making, understanding, and valuing music.

Figure 8.1 represents the various aspects of content in music. The horizontal lines through the middle of the figure mark the distinction between activities (the things people do with music) and outcomes (the things that tend to be remembered about music). The activities of performing, listening, creating, reading, and describing or analyzing are related through connecting lines to each other and to making, understanding and knowing, and valuing music.

Figure 8.1   The Various Aspects of Content in Music

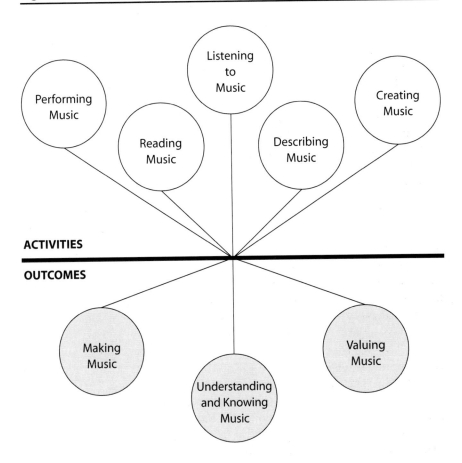

Attitudes

How a person feels about what he or she knows is important. This statement is truer for music than for most academic subjects. All of us use the ability to read and write daily, regardless of whether or not we enjoyed reading or writing when we were taught them in school. We need to balance checkbooks and compute income taxes, regardless of how we feel about arithmetic.

Not so with music. People who don't like music can refrain from streaming music and attending concerts. If forced to listen to music at a supermarket, they can mentally tune it out. Much of the ultimate success of music instruction depends on how the students feel about the subject after classes are over. And students do acquire attitudes about music, whether or not teachers realize it. The question is not, "Will students develop feelings about music?" Rather, it is, "What attitudes about music will students develop?"

Attitudes and knowledge are complementary. People cannot have intelligent reactions to something they don't know. If asked, "Do you like aardvarks?" your answer will probably be, "I don't know." A teacher's first task is to remove ignorance so that at least there can be intelligent preferences, and at best there can be what educator-philosopher Harry Broudy referred to as "enlightened cherishing" (Broudy, 1968). Few people, including music teachers, enjoy all types of music. Being educated about something does not mean that you must like it. Rather, education should offer people the opportunity to make intelligent musical choices, even if deep down their music teachers really want them to enjoy it.

What influences the attitudes people adopt? Some generalizations can be offered in terms of tendencies, but no rules can be stated that people always follow. One generalization concerns familiarity. If there be truth in the statement, "I know what I like," there is also truth in the words, "I like what I know." Social scientists have discovered this fact in a variety of situations ranging from people to words to pictures. People tend to like things that are similar to what they already know and like. A person who likes Broadway musicals can more easily acquire a favorable attitude toward concert music than can someone who refuses to listen to anything except rap or heavy metal.

People are influenced by the person who suggests change. A teacher who is liked is more effective in changing attitudes than one who isn't. Part of the reason for this lies in the fact that students have a pleasant association with the subject when they like the teacher.

Attitudes are also influenced by what friends and peers think. This is especially true of students in their adolescent years. If all their friends like a particular piece of music, chances are greatly increased that other students will like it too. This is true partly because they respect and like their friends, partly because they don't want the friction involved in disagreeing with them, and partly because they tend to "go with the flow" of their feelings as they perceive them.

The family has a significant influence on children's attitudes. If the parents listen to symphonies on their quality sound system at home, the chances are much greater that the children will end up listening to that type of music when they are mature.

GUIDELINES FOR THE CONTENT OF MUSIC CLASSES AND REHEARSALS

Because time is so often limited for music instruction, teachers must make careful decisions about what to teach. In doing so, they may consult students, parents, and curriculum guides. Even when they do these things, they still have to make choices. The following guidelines can help in doing this.

Educational. The first guideline is basic: Students should gain information, skills, or attitudes that they probably did not have prior to the class or course and may not acquire without instruction in school. Otherwise, education becomes merely babysitting or a recreational program. Although this important guideline is a simple one, it is not always followed. Sometimes teachers feel the effort to teach something is not worth it, or that it will not make any difference to the students. Whatever the reason, the students are the losers.

Valid. Music is an established academic discipline, a recognized field of knowledge and study. Teachers should ask themselves, "Is what is being taught a legitimate part of the field of music as recognized and accepted by most trained performers, musicologists, and teachers?" For example, a few teachers of violin with elementary school children use a kind of notation in which notes are identified not by pitch but rather by the name of the strings and fingerings—A1, D3, and so on. The system cannot indicate relative pitch, note values, or sharps and flats. It must be unlearned when a student progresses. No music theorist, symphony musician, or musicologist uses this system in studying or playing music. Therefore, it is not valid. The call for validity is a logical one. It is neither logical nor honest to transform a subject, even in the hope of aiding learning.

Fundamental. Closely related to validity of content is the belief that students should learn the basic ideas of the subject, not just factual minutiae. Knowing the keys of the thirty-two Beethoven piano sonatas is clearly not as useful as understanding the concept of development of themes and motives. When information is associated with a concept, it is useful. Having students memorize insignificant facts is not effective teaching. Fundamental ideas—tonality, phrasing, the 2:1 ratio in rhythmic notation, and the unity of words and music in art songs, to cite a few examples that are valuable because they are comprehensive and have wide application in music.

Representative. If the music curriculum is limited to only a few types or aspects of music, then students are not being given a well-balanced education in music. The band director who has the band learn only one or two marching shows a year and the general music teacher who spends almost all the class time working with computers are shortchanging their students because both omit many of the other areas of music. Sometimes teachers give students very little concert music—music that contains a more sophisticated handling of sounds. Their students continue to think of music only as a pastime or entertainment. They are not exposed to the idea of music as an aesthetic, expressive human creation.

Contemporary. Music and information taught in music classes should be up to date. This criterion refers not only to the date when composed but also to the style. Some works composed in the last thirty years are still in a style that is a century old. The main obstacle for teachers in this matter is the technical difficulty of many contemporary works. Many music teachers would like to have their students sing or play music in a contemporary style, but often the works are too difficult. It requires some searching, but contemporary works that are not overly demanding can be found.

Relevant. When the interests of the students and the requirements of valid subject matter are in conflict, advocates of relevance ask, "What good is a subject that seems meaningless and worthless to the students?" This view has a fair claim for the attention of teachers. Part of their job may be making something seem relevant to their students. Relevance is probably affected more by the method of teaching than by the content. A topic that is important and interesting to one person couldn't matter less to another.

Relevance results when a topic is given meaning through a teacher's attitude and skill in organizing and presenting the subject.

Teachers need to teach so the content of the music class becomes relevant to the students. For example, figuring out the three forms of minor scales is not relevant to most students because it does not particularly help their understanding of music. But having the students hear a song in a major key and then in a minor key helps them appreciate the effect the change of mode can have. Achieving relevance is a challenging assignment.

Learnable. The music curriculum must be learnable by most of the students. It is useless to teach something for which they are not prepared. Although the students' backgrounds and interests should be considered, these are not the only factors teachers should think about. Teaching a piece of music that is a suitable level of difficulty for the students should be determined in relation to the other guidelines, as well as to a host of practical matters such as amount of class time, books and materials, and performance obligations. A capable teacher can build on the interests students already have without abandoning the subject. If students seem uninterested in a worthwhile topic, perhaps another approach to it is called for instead of giving up on it entirely.

Some of the guidelines presented here may appear to be contradictory, and to a degree they are. The need to offer substantive instruction seems to work against the idea of relevancy, and contemporary content may appear to contradict the idea of representative samples of the subject. In the case of education versus relevancy, the solution lies in the proper methods of teaching. Teachers, however, need to strike a balance in making curricular decisions among conflicting needs. None of these guidelines are absolute and overriding.

National, State, and Local Guidelines

Because music is a specialized area, its teachers, especially at the secondary school level, have a great deal of freedom in deciding what they teach and when to teach it. This has both desirable and undesirable aspects. On one hand, teachers often have the freedom to decide the content of their classes and rehearsals. They can tailor their instruction to suit the particular situation, as well as their personal preferences. On the other hand, they have little guidance and help in making those decisions.

Some guidance for teachers of general music classes in elementary schools may be found in the general and curriculum guides created by states, and a few school districts include detailed plans and much more material than can ever be covered, even in the rare instance of a ninety-minute long class. Furthermore, curriculum guides are rarely created for performing ensembles. Only the 2014 national standards have attempted to provide guidance for courses in the secondary schools. Usually, the only guidance for ensemble directors consists of a few requirements and lists of acceptable music that state festival organizations have created. These come in the form of requirements for festival participation such as specified scales and sight- reading, plus a list of approved music for various classifications of ensembles.

Technological Advances

Recent technological developments are having a major impact on what and how music can be taught. One important change is the thousands of YouTube examples of music being performed and in some cases explained and demonstrated. They range from how a harpsichord makes sounds to outstanding performances of almost all types of music by both amateur and highly esteemed performers. Permission has been cleared for all the examples. The visual and sound quality of the recordings varies, with the more recent recordings usually having clearly superior visuals and sound. YouTube examples can bring to life in classrooms such diverse things as drumming by African drummers and performances by outstanding concert pianists and violinists. No longer are teachers limited to what students can read in a book or just listen to on individual audio recordings.

YouTube examples are not without risk, however. They can be withdrawn without notice if there is a copyright or other challenge to a video. This means that occasionally an excellent video will no longer be available. When this happens the good news is that the topics of most videos can be replaced by one or more of the similar videos that are available. While the new video may lack one or two of the features that attracted the teacher to the first choice, it can usually be replaced.

The attractive educational possibilities of videos has encouraged the production of special ones that deal with aspects of music in imaginative ways. The former basal book series has been greatly expanded and enriched to take advantage of the opportunities offered by technology.

A recent example of using technology in teaching instrumental music is a program called SmartMusic. The music for beginning and intermediate method books has been captured in video form for individual students to use for a fee of about $40 a year per student. In this program, students examine an assigned example from the particular book for each of them to record. When they enter the assigned example, the computer presents it in sound with notation. Students can listen to and follow the example alone as many times as they wish.

When students think they are ready, they record their performance of the example. They then see what they played on the monitor. Any errors in pitch or rhythm are indicated in red notes. Students can play the example again, presumably with the errors reduced or eliminated. When satisfied with their performances, they can email it to their teachers, who can listen to and evaluate each student's performance at their convenience. Usually students record their performances at home or individually in a practice room.

Granted, the computer cannot teach the physical actions needed for playing an instrument. It can, however, be of much help in teaching students to play the right notes at the right time.

QUESTIONS

1. What five things could students in a band learn in conjunction with "The Stars and Stripes Forever" by Sousa, in addition to playing the right notes at the right time?
2. Think of examples of three different types of musical skills.
3. Why is a sense of musical syntax so important in learning music?
4. What is a concept?
5. Why should students develop concepts about music?
6. How does musician-like thinking about the song "Simple Gifts" differ from everyday, ordinary thinking about it?
7. Why is it very desirable for students in music classes to acquire favorable attitudes toward the subject?
8. What factors affect the attitudes people adopt toward music?
9. What does the word "relevant" mean in discussions of curriculum?

PROJECTS

1. Select a piece of music for use with a class or performing group. List what students could learn from studying it.
2. Select another musical work. Describe why it is or could be valid, fundamental, and relevant.

REFERENCES

Broudy, H. S. (1968). The case for aesthetic education. In R. A. Choate (Ed.), *Documentary report of the Tanglewood symposium* (p. 13). Reston, VA: Music Educators National Conference.

Kurst-Wilson, W. R., & Zajonc, R. B. (1980). Affective discrimination of stimuli that cannot be recognized. *Science, 207,* 557–558.

Oléron, P. (1977). *Language and mental development* (R. P. Lorion, Trans.). Hillsdale, NJ: Lawrence Erlbaum.

Penfield, W., & Roberts, T. (1959). *Speech and brain-mechanisms.* Princeton, NJ: Princeton University Press.

The Elementary School Music Program

It is important for prospective teachers to be informed about and interested in the entire school music program—kindergarten through high school, general, choral, and instrumental. The reason for an interest in the total program is the fact that it is a single entity. At each level or in each type of class, students learn music, and each portion of the music program affects the other parts to some degree.

GOALS OF THE ELEMENTARY SCHOOL MUSIC PROGRAM

The same basic goals prevail for all components and levels of the music education program. The amount of attention devoted to certain goals vary according to the type of class, but that does not change the fact that the entire program is (or should be) related and coordinated from one portion to another.

Over the decades, various committees and symposia have developed sets of goals for elementary school music education. They differ in number and specifics, but there is a general consensus that the following six goals are important for all students. The ability to:

- sing reasonably well,
- play a simple instrument,
- create simple music by improvising or composing,
- listen to music perceptively,

- know basic information about music, including music notation, and

- value and discriminate with respect to music.

At first glance, some of the goals may seem unrealistic for some levels. Considered carefully, however, they are not. For example, playing an instrument can be as simple as rendering a tune on a mallet instrument, and creating music can consist of making up a short introduction to a song. Basic information includes such points as knowing the part of the world a piece of music comes from and if it contains a pattern such as A-B-A. And, yes, by the time students finish their years in elementary school, they should have a rudimentary knowledge of music notation.

Most college students have only vague memories of their instruction in music back when they were eight or ten years old. In many cases, they didn't receive much music instruction in school, so there isn't much to remember. In other cases, the passage of ten or more years has dimmed their memory of what took place. What memories they have may consist mostly of singing songs. The experiences of the musicals and contest/festivals in high school seem fresher and more interesting.

Music classes in elementary schools are not only at least as important in terms of education as are the performing groups, but they also can be musically rewarding experiences for everyone. The author once heard a musicologist ridicule music in the elementary schools as just the singing of songs like "The Little Red Caboose." His inaccurate perception is probably shared by others when they think about music in the elementary schools. If this view of music at that level was ever accurate—and it probably was at some time in some places—it is certainly not a correct one today.

To begin, the content of the classes consists of much more than singing songs. Step into an elementary classroom during music. You may see students creating pieces out of sounds they find around the room. You may observe them listening to and then analyzing a short work by Mozart or Villa-Lobos or an African percussion piece. Or you may see students working with classroom instruments to gain a better feel for patterns of pitch and rhythm. And yes, you may listen to them sing some songs, including songs in the popular idiom, folk songs, and a few classical songs. If an elementary school music class is dull, it's the fault of the teacher who is not taking advantage of the myriad of musical possibilities available to them.

The claim here is not that music in elementary or middle schools operates at the same technical level as high school performing groups.

The difficulty level of the music is only one aspect of music, however. A well-shaped phrase and expressive performance can happen just as easily in simple music as it can in complex works (and maybe more easily). When performed expressively, William Billing's "Chester" is a stirring work, whether it is sung by a classroom of fifth graders or played by a high school band as arranged by William Schuman. Musical satisfaction comes from the expressive qualities of the music, not from its technical difficulty. Because music is music regardless of its difficulty, teaching music in the elementary schools can be musically very satisfying.

IMPORTANCE OF THE ELEMENTARY PROGRAM

The reasons for the importance of the general or classroom music program are compelling. First and most important, it is the portion of the music curriculum that involves every student. For many of them it is the only formal instruction they will ever receive in music.

Second, the general music program represents the foundation on which subsequent efforts in music are built. A child who had a hard time carrying a tune in primary grades and developed doubts and fears about his or her musical ability is not a good candidate for high school choir or band. And in later years, he or she is unlikely to be supportive of music in the schools as a voter, principal, or school board member. For these two perhaps selfish reasons, music educators should seek to have a strong and successful music program in the elementary schools.

Research in how children acquire language skills has strongly supported the importance of children learning language and singing even before they enter school. Unfortunately, American children do not enter kindergarten until they are five years old. Language development has already passed the time when it has probably reached its acme. In any case, the more experiences in matching pitch and recognizing differences in what they hear, the better it is. Granted, the songs are short and simple, but they are vital to the development of a foundation for success in music.

In spite of its importance and musical validity, restricted school budgets have placed elementary school music programs in danger of being nibbled away through reductions in instructional time, number of teachers, and funds for books and other materials. The reason for this situation is partly due to a lack of visibility. General music classes cannot (and should not) enter festivals and contests in which they are rated. Nor do such classes have booster groups raising funds for them, as desirable as that might be. These classes simply do not have the benefit of public awareness associated with performing ensembles. This situation is also partly due to a lack of awareness on the part of school administrators about the scope and value of the general music program. If music were just singing some songs, as many people erroneously believe, then reducing the amount of time for music instruction merely means singing a few less songs. It's not a serious matter in their minds.

Another drawback concerns false ideas held by many non-musicians about music and talent. The popular view is this: If a person has "it" (talent), then music study is worthwhile. For most people—those with average or modest talent—it really doesn't matter much whether they receive instruction in music. Of course, it would be wonderful if everyone supported music for all students and understood the value of music education. For now, and for the foreseeable future, teachers of general music need to work hard to present their efforts publicly and to educate school administrators and the community about the nature and the value of music for all students.

Types of Situations

Most of the music program in elementary schools consists of classroom music. That is, music is taught to all of the children in a particular classroom at the same time for the purpose of educating them in music, not just to prepare them for performances. It is required of all students and is general in nature, which implies a wide variety of activities and content.

Many elementary schools also offer some music activities on an extracurricular basis. Probably the most frequent offering of this type is a choral group for students in the upper grades. Sometimes it meets during school time, but more often it utilizes a lunch hour or a recess. Some schools offer recorder classes on this basis. The method of allowing students to join such groups is by a student's expression of interest, a "selection-by-election" approach. Students are not usually auditioned for membership in elementary school music groups, although some music teachers believe that only students who pass an audition should be members.

Instrumental music is offered in many districts at about the fifth- or sixth-grade level. Many schools allow any interested student to begin instrumental study, but in other schools the size of the beginning classes is limited. In such cases, teachers select the students who will be allowed to begin instrumental study. Sometimes aptitude tests are used for screening purposes, and in other cases reports and recommendations of the students' school music teachers are considered. In some school districts students are allowed to start instrumental study in a summer program, and only those students who show sufficient interest and ability are allowed to continue in the fall.

Traditionally, families of instruments are taught together, such as all wind or string instruments. Instrumental instruction is done by an instrumental music specialist who travels among several elementary schools or by an instrumental specialist at the middle school level. These classes meet twice a week for thirty or forty minutes in elementary schools. The students are excused from classroom activities according to the instrumental music teacher's schedule. In middle schools, the beginning instrumental classes are part of the schedule, which may meet daily or every other day in a block schedule. The classes tend to be small (ten to fifteen students) in elementary school situations. Instrumental classes are often much larger in middle schools.

Amount of Time

A typical schedule for music instruction for elementary school classroom music is once a week for forty minutes, although there are sizable differences throughout the United States. NAfME recommends ninety minutes per week. Most of the elective extracurricular music activities are on a twice-a-week basis. A few schools allow for some individualized learning activities.

Personnel Responsible for Music Instruction

Music specialists and consultants are teachers who are certified in the area of music. They majored in music in college, took methods courses, and had student teaching experience that qualified them for certification as music teachers. Clearly, music specialists are strong in subject matter preparation. They are not always assigned to just one school, but like the instrumental music teachers, sometimes travel among two or more buildings. They are responsible for only one subject: music. This has its advantages and disadvantages.

The difference, if any, between music specialists and music consultants is the implication that consultants are more likely to spend time helping classroom teachers to teach music. Actually, many people use the terms specialist and consultant interchangeably. The problem for consultants is that, except by a few teachers who are already strong in music, their help is not requested nearly enough. Teachers who don't want to draw attention to their lack of knowledge of the subject seldom call on the consultant. Consultants have no administrative authority. In some cases, a consultant is responsible for a number of schools, which makes it difficult to have much personal contact with the classroom teachers. Written curriculum guides and memos must take the place of personal contacts. Sometimes consultants organize in-service instruction for teachers in a building or district. These sessions not only help the teachers to teach music better, they also aid in improving communication and coordination among the different types of teachers.

Music supervisors are more likely to work with music specialists as administrators in the subject area of music, although the term "supervisor" is sometimes used as a synonym for consultant.

MUSIC AND CLASSROOM TEACHERS

Classroom teachers hold a college degree in elementary education. One or two music courses are part of their undergraduate preparation, so their music training is very limited. Usually they are responsible for most of the instruction their students receive in school. The curricular areas for which they are sometimes not always responsible include physical education, art, and music. They enjoy some advantages over music specialists in teaching music. They know the students in their classrooms very well, and they can be more flexible about working music into the classroom routine. If ten o'clock is the best time to study the music of sailors, then it can take place at that time. If the study of sailors is to be led by a music specialist, it will have to wait until the specialist's scheduled time. Furthermore, classroom teachers can integrate subject matter better because they teach most of the subjects.

Classroom teachers are at a disadvantage in terms of their knowledge and ability in music. Activities that require on-the-spot musical judgments are difficult for most classroom teachers. In addition, although they may know their twenty-plus students well, they have little concept of the entire music program as it applies to other grade levels. This situation, along with their incomplete preparation in music, prompted the Teacher Education Commission of NAfME to recommend that music in elementary schools be taught by music specialists (Klotman, 1972).

Over the years, the music education profession has changed its opinion about the role of classroom teachers in teaching music. In the 1940s and 1950s, the profession promoted the idea of music teaching by classroom teachers. The 1960s saw a trend toward subject-matter emphasis and a corresponding movement away from what was termed the "self-contained classroom." It prompted the profession to retreat from the view that the classroom teacher could and should teach music.

This change of attention to subject matter content was not the only reason for less emphasis on music teaching by classroom teachers. Music educators began to realize that classroom teachers have a difficult time preparing for all the subjects they teach. Classroom teachers usually save for last the preparing of "special" subjects like music.

Although classroom teachers may no longer carry the brunt of the music instruction, they are still important to the success of the program in the elementary schools, for several reasons. First, there are simply not enough music specialists to take care of all the music instruction that is needed; classroom teachers need to take up the slack.

Second, the attitude of classroom teachers toward music is very important to the success of the program, even if they don't actually teach the music themselves. All teachers, whether they realize it or not, serve as behavior models for their students. Elementary school students are quick to detect and are influenced by their teachers' attitudes toward music. When a music specialist visits the classroom, a lack of interest and support from the classroom teacher can undercut what the specialist tries to accomplish. Some classroom teachers welcome the arrival of the specialist and hurry off to the teachers' lounge. Others say, "It's not time for music A-GAIN, is it?" Occasionally, classroom teachers turn over unruly classes to music specialists with words such as, "They're really climbing the walls today. Lotsa luck!"

Third, classroom teachers can follow up the efforts of music specialists in many ways. For example, they can have the children review a song on a day when the specialist is not in the building or listen to the rest of a recording that was begun during the music lesson. Children benefit from limited amounts of daily work in skill areas such as reading or singing, and classroom teachers are the only persons who can provide daily practice. Such follow-up is vital because, as pointed out earlier, even when music specialists are responsible for the music instruction, the amount of time for music is restricted.

Combination Arrangements for Instruction

It is difficult to secure up-to-date and accurate figures on who is responsible for music instruction in the elementary schools. There are many variations from state to state and district to district, and some confusion exists about the terminology for designating the roles of teachers. One nationwide study reported that 45 percent of all school districts are served by full-time music specialists, 39 percent by part-time specialists, and 16 percent have no music specialists (MENC, 1990).

Content of Classroom Instruction

The material taught in music classes in elementary classrooms is general in nature. A wide variety of topics and activities is included, and none is taught in much depth because of limited time. Basically, students learn about music and its constituent parts (melody, rhythm, timbre, form, and so on) by becoming involved in basic musical processes (performing, creating, and analyzing). The traditional division of the elementary school music program was by the activities associated with basic musical processes: singing, playing instruments, rhythmic movement, creating, and reading as a part of performing, and listening as the activity associated with analyzing.

The actual content included under the various classifications can be best observed in the graded music series books and materials for use in the elementary schools. Two publishers currently market attractive series of comprehensive materials designed for use in elementary schools: Macmillan/McGraw Hill's "Spotlight on Music" and Silver Burdett/Pearson's "SmartMusic." These materials contain many similarities, although there are a number of subtle and perhaps significant differences between them. They are filled with color illustrations and their content is carefully prepared with the help of expert consultants to ensure accuracy and suitability for the grade level. Each series includes many ideas and suggestions for the teachers and recordings of all the music presented in each level, with songs sung by children.

Traditionally, the books were mostly songbooks, but as the nature of the elementary music program has expanded, so has the variety of material. Books designed for the second grade typically contain many songs, of which about half are folk songs. In addition, there are listening sections, charts, creative activities, parts for classroom instruments such as autoharp, assessment materials, ideas from the Orff and Kodály programs, presentations of styles in music and the other arts, and suggestions for mainstreaming children with disabilities. Books for fifth graders contain more songs, including part songs, and present more advanced material similar to what is contained in the second grade level.

Although not mandatory for teaching music, these materials make an excellent starting place of creative ideas and useful materials from which teachers can build a program. Their benefits are numerous:

- They are a source of songs and other musical activities so that a teacher is spared the effort of searching for appropriate materials and ideas.
- They provide a course of study in music for each grade level. In fact, the Silver Burdett materials include thirty-six lessons, one for each week in a school year.
- The teacher's editions of each book suggest teaching procedures. Reference material is included, and songs and learning activities are thoroughly indexed.
- Ideas for incorporating classroom instruments and orchestral instruments into accompaniments are provided.
- Pronunciation guides for all foreign language songs are included. Translations are also provided if they are not already contained in the verses of the song.
- The recorded performances are high in quality and the caliber of the singing, usually done by children, is excellent. They provide a good model of singing for children to emulate.
- Suggestions are offered for extending learning activities into other arts and other subject matter areas, including help for students with disabilities. For teachers using the approaches devised by Carl Orff and Zoltan Kodály (see Chapter 11), there are recommendations for incorporating those teaching techniques into music instruction.
- Many activities are suggested to make music classes more engaging and varied. These include scripts for plays, games, listening guides, materials for bulletin boards, recorder and guitar music, and copy masters of various items.
- Assistance is provided for assessing learning in music classes.

Music for students in elementary schools can be truly interesting and educationally significant. The materials for achieving new and different music lessons are available to help teachers provide a quality experience with music.

QUESTIONS

1. Why is the general music program at the elementary level an important and essential part of the school music program?
2. Why does the general music program sometimes suffer when it comes to funding?
3. What does a typical music program at the elementary school level consist of in terms of types of teachers, instruction offered, amount of time, students involved, and materials used?
4. What are the advantages of having music in elementary schools taught by music specialists?
5. What are the advantages of having music in elementary schools taught by classroom teachers?
6. What are the benefits of using materials from one of the graded music series?

REFERENCES

Klotman, R. H. (Ed.). (1972). *Teacher education in music: Final report.* Reston, VA: Music Educators National Conference.
Market Data Retrieval. (2007). *Number of music teachers in public and private schools K–12.* www.schooldata.com
Music Educators National Conference (MENC). (1986). *Guidelines for performances of school music groups: Expectations and limitations.* Reston, VA: Author.
Music Educators National Conference (MENC). (1990). *Data on music education.* Reston, VA: Author.
Soundpost, 3(8) (Spring 1992), 9.

The Secondary School Music Program

School music programs face a clear divide between the elementary and secondary levels. The classroom program involving all the students normally concludes with fifth grade. Usually there is one more general course in sixth or seventh grade that involves many of the students. Those who are not in that general course have elected instrumental or vocal music. For most students the general course concludes their education in music. At the age of 12, their music instruction in school is over.

No uniform national pattern exists for schools containing grades 5 or 6 through 9. There are middle schools composed of grades 5 through 8 or 6 through 8, and junior high schools consisting of grades 7 and 8 or 7 through 9. Some one-grade level schools also exist. In addition, there are "magnet" or special-emphasis schools at both the middle and high school levels (Goffe, 1991).

In many ways, music education in secondary schools is a very different world from its elementary school counterpart. Most of the program, especially at the high school level, consists of performing groups. Music courses are almost entirely elective, involving only a small minority of the students—about one out of five or six. Yet the secondary school program is far more visible than the elementary school program. In fact, the high school performing groups are the only portion of the program that most of the public ever sees. These groups often enter contests and festivals, and many of them have booster organizations.

GENERAL MUSIC

American music education has an enviable record in terms of producing outstanding performing groups at the secondary school level, especially bands. But its accomplishments in the teaching of most students in its secondary schools are not as impressive. Part of the reason for this discrepancy between performance and nonperformance courses lies in the interest music teachers have shown in the two areas. Some teachers consider the general music class as a feeder program for high school organizations. Others see it as a recreational period in which it doesn't much matter if the students learn a lot. Many teachers assigned to general music classes would rather be directing high school groups, and so they simply do not give such classes much attention or thought. As a result, general music has been reduced or eliminated in many junior high and middle schools.

Accurate data are hard to come by for music in middle schools, but the trend seems to be downward. Many middle schools have relegated general music to a set of "exploratory" courses that all sixth or seventh grade students take in one course that is only six or nine weeks long. That course is the total middle school music experience for most students. This rotation of electives, sometimes called the "wheel," provides a very limited education in music.

In some school systems, the general music course in middle school is the first instruction in music the students receive from a music specialist. In other school systems, the students have a strong background in music because of their elementary school experiences. The size of general music classes varies. Usually they are the same size as other academic classes, but in a few cases they contain sixty or more students.

The content of the general music classes at the middle school level differs somewhat from music instruction at the elementary level in terms of the attention given to the various aspects of music instruction. Although some singing and other music-making activities are continued, more time and effort is devoted to listening and analyzing. There are at least two reasons for the increased emphasis on listening in these classes. One is that many of the boys undergo a change of voice in their early teen years, and singing is not as easy or satisfying during the transition. A second and more important reason is that after the students finish their schooling, the main contact most of them will have with music will be as listeners. Therefore, music teachers try to help students improve their skill in listening to music.

Although listening receives more attention in middle school general music classes, singing and other types of music making should still be continued. General music should not become a class in which students only listen to and talk about music.

ELECTIVE COURSES

Data reveal that the enrollment in high school music courses is heavily concentrated in band, with choral music about 15 percent smaller. Band enrollment is about seven times larger than that for orchestra. Enrollments in general music, music appreciation, and advanced placement courses in music make up less than 5 percent of all the music enrollments, leaving more than 95 percent in performance groups (MDR, 2007). Clearly, the music curriculum at the high school level is overwhelmingly focused on performing organizations.

Although performing groups dominate the music program in America's high schools, music educators should not forget about music theory, music appreciation, and fine arts courses, as well as advance placement courses. They should do what they reasonably can to bring the performance and nonperformance aspects of the program into better balance. Often this balance can be partially corrected when nonperformance courses are offered in the school curriculum and promoted among the students. When teachers have the opportunity to teach such a course, they should devote as much effort to the course as they give to their performing groups.

REASONS FOR DOMINANCE OF PERFORMING GROUPS

Why is the secondary school music program so performance oriented? It began with the great leap forward in secondary school enrollments that occurred between the years 1910 and 1940. Such an increase meant that many of the students going to high school were not college-bound, which had been the role of high school educations. A greater variety of courses was needed in the curriculum. Also, attitudes changed about the value of subjects beyond the traditional academic ones.

The rapid expansion of school music at the secondary level also meant there were not enough trained music teachers at that level, so schools had to turn to professional musicians to teach music. Their opportunities to make a living as performers were waning because of The Great Depression and sound movies. In turn, the former professional musicians, naturally, worked with their secondary school performing groups in much the same way as a director of a professional ensemble. The period when the ensemble met was called a "rehearsal," and its purpose was to prepare for performances. The teacher was des-

Figure 10.1   Music Programs at American Schools

	Music Program		
	Required	**Elective**	**Selective**
Elementary School	General Music	Choral groups Instrumental Study	
Middle School/ Junior High School	General Music	Choral Groups Instrumental Classes Beginning Intermediate	Choir Band Jazz Band Orchestra
Senior High School		Applied Music Appreciation Fine Arts Theory Choral Groups Voice Classes	Choir Band Jazz Band Orchestra
Extra-curricular (after school, no credit)		Music Clubs Small Ensembles Musical Shows Pep Band Jazz Band Marching Band Auxiliary Units	

ignated "director," a term more familiar to professional musicians. For these reasons, music in high schools became the only curricular area in which "directors" conducted "rehearsals" instead of teachers who teach classes.

There are several solid reasons for continuing performing groups in the secondary schools. One is that students learn by doing and experiencing. Students who go through the effort of learning their parts and rehearsing with the group know a musical work much more thoroughly than students who only listen to it. Another positive feature of performing groups is that they fulfill the teenage need for recognition and activity. In most of their other school courses, students sit passively. Music is one area in which they can truly participate. Preparing music for a performance motivates them and offers them a chance for recognition. A third reason in favor of performing groups is that they are well established in the school curriculum. Teachers are trained in teaching them and good materials are available. There is also an important fourth reason for performing groups: They provide much visibility for one aspect of the music program.

The professional musicians who entered the teaching field made valuable contributions to music education. Even today, the limited opportunities for making a living as a performer have turned many toward education. Common interests bind professional musicians and music educators together, and the teaching profession needs capable and sensitive musicians. What should be realized, however, is that what is good for a professional organization is often not the best one for school groups. Because the two groups exist for different purposes, they need to be approached differently.

Furthermore, what continues to be needed is a building of nonperformance courses and an evolution toward more educationally valid performing groups. Ways of increasing the amount and type of learning in performing groups, which are beyond the scope of this book, are presented in the author's *Teaching Music in the Secondary Schools, 5/E.*

TYPES OF PERFORMING GROUPS

Students want and need music instruction that is suited to their abilities and interests. Whenever enrollments permit, groups that are designed for varying levels of ability should be available for students to join. For example, there could be a choir for more interested and talented students and a chorus for less able and interested students.

Teachers need to guard against slighting the less talented. The education given students in a chorus is just as important as the education given students in the best choir.

Small Ensembles

A weakness of music education at the secondary school level is its lopsided emphasis on large ensembles. Music educators realize that performing in small ensembles is a valuable experience for students. They gain independence by usually being the only performer on a part. Small ensemble experience also engenders interest and musicianship. In addition, there is a rich literature for combinations involving strings and groups such as woodwind quintets and brass ensembles. Many include piano.

Several factors discourage small ensembles in the schools, however. To begin, it is hard to work up public enthusiasm for a woodwind quintet or horn trio, which is not true for large ensembles. Second, the time that teachers can devote to small ensembles is limited. Their schedules are filled with classes and large ensemble rehearsals. Few school systems can afford to hire a teacher for classes of only four or five students. Lastly, the amount of time available to students for small ensembles is limited as well. Only a few students have time in their school schedules for more than one music class, and that class usually is a large ensemble. Most small ensembles are formed for purposes of performing at an adjudicated contest or music festival, and they can meet only a few times with a teacher.

These problems do not erase the fact that small ensemble experience is highly desirable. Some teachers arrange for several small ensembles to rehearse at the same time in adjacent rooms so they can circulate among the groups. In some situations, the better performers form an ensemble. Because they learn their parts more quickly than the other students, they can be excused from part of a large ensemble rehearsal once or twice a week to rehearse small ensemble music.

Orchestras

For a variety of reasons, orchestras have been far surpassed in enrollment by bands. This is unfortunate for two reasons. First, the orchestral literature is much richer. Very few of the major composers throughout music history have written for bands. Except for a limited number of contemporary works, bands must play transcriptions or pieces written for the educational market, which are not usually as desirable as the original works. The wind band is slowly acquiring quality contemporary literature of its own, and possibly in fifty years the problem of literature will not be as serious. Second, the playing opportunities after high school for interested amateurs lie overwhelmingly in orchestras, which use only a limited number of winds.

Band directors give three reasons for not offering string instruction: (1) it will take potentially good players away from the band, resulting in two mediocre ensembles instead of one good one; (2) there is no string specialist in the district; and (3) the band director has no time for any more classes. The first reason may have some truth to it in school districts with enrollments of less than 1,000 for grades 7 through 12. However, some small districts have a good band and a good orchestra. The excuse of a lack of string teaching ability is not valid. Band directors who are clarinet players do not hesitate teaching brass instruments, at least at the beginning and intermediate levels.

The matter of teacher time must be examined. It is not possible to get something for nothing. Fortunately, school-quality string instruments cost about the same as wind instruments. They can be rented from music merchants, in which case a sizable investment by the school district is not required. During the first year or two in which a string program is introduced, only a small amount of additional teacher time is needed.

Marching Bands

The marching band has its commendable features. It is good public relations for the music department. Many people see the band only at football games or a parade, which often makes it their only contact with the school music program. Its members achieve recognition, school spirit is fostered, and good feelings are generated all around as the colorful group parades by. What could anyone have against something that gives so many people enjoyment and leaves them impressed with the school music program?

The problem is that in some communities the marching band has dominated the music program. In fact, in some high schools the marching band has become almost the entire music program. The result is a very limited music education for a modest number of students and just about no music instruction for the vast majority of students.

The problem has been intensified in many places because of the growth of marching band contests and the increasing popularity of the corps style of marching. Students in corps-style bands usually learn only one or two shows a year and perform that show for every appearance, thereby further restricting their musical experience. Many of the appearances are at marching band contests, with some bands entering three or more contests each fall. The evaluation of bands at these contests is based partially on nonmusical factors. Furthermore, a positive correlation seems to exist between the size of the group (band members and auxiliary units) and the ratings received.

What can band directors do about the situation? In most American communities today, the marching band is so much a part of the scene that it is unrealistic to suggest that it be discontinued, which would not be a good idea anyway. Teachers can begin by bringing the attention devoted to the marching band into proportion with that given other aspects of the music program. Such an adjustment may mean reducing the number of appearances or contests entered. It may mean simplifying the marching shows in terms of the routines the students are expected to learn. (In any case, most football fans cannot tell the difference between a complicated and a simple band show.) A third action that will make the teachers' lives a little easier is to have someone else oversee the auxiliary units—flag bearers, rifle corps, pom-pom unit, and so on. When other teachers or people in the community work with these groups, this allows directors to devote more time to other aspects of their work.

Jazz Bands and Swing Choirs

Should specialized performing groups such as jazz bands, madrigal singers, and swing choirs be included in the secondary school curriculum on the same basis as band, orchestra, choir, and general music? Such groups should be offered when possible, but they should be operated as adjuncts to the larger groups. For example, jazz band membership should be made available only to the students who are members of the concert band or to those who have been members for two or more years. This principle is promoted by MENC (1986). Figures 10.2 and 10.3 present charts for band and choir that depict ensembles ancillary to the main organization.

The reason for this recommendation concerns the quality of the education that students receive in music. A student's musical education is limited by his or her premature selection of one specialized area before becoming educated about the larger world of band music. In some schools, such specialized groups have received most of the attention by the teacher and the public, while the effort devoted to the larger group has been reduced.

Music teachers in many states are certified for all school grades. Even when not certified for all levels, they should realize that they are part of a large and varied program of instruction. Music programs should be a coordinated and planned effort from kindergarten through grade 12.

Figure 10.2   Concert Choir and Related Groups

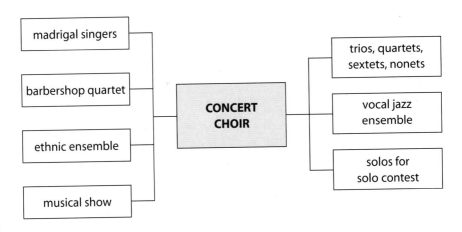

Figure 10.3   Concert Band and Related Groups

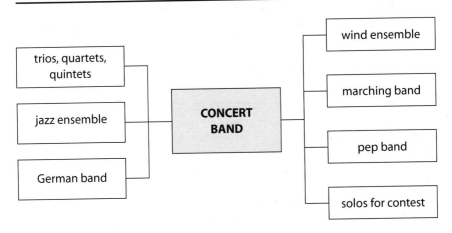

QUESTIONS

1. What are some of the reasons why music course offerings in American high schools consist largely of performing groups?
2. Why should small ensemble experiences be provided for students in secondary school performing groups?
3. Why should a string orchestra be included in the school music curriculum?
4. In addition to playing or singing the right notes at the right time, what should students in ensembles learn when studying a piece of music?
5. At what grade level does all the music instruction in school end for most students?

REFERENCES

Goffe, J. (1991). Music programs in performing arts high schools: Current status and implications for future development. Unpublished doctoral dissertation, University of Florida.

Klotman, R. H. (Ed.). (1972). *Teacher education in music: Final report.* Reston, VA: Music Educators National Conference.

Market Data Retrieval. (2007). *Number of music teachers in public and private schools K–12.* www.schooldata.com

Music Educators National Conference (MENC). (1986). *Guidelines for performances of school music groups: Expectations and limitations.* Reston, VA: Author.

Music Educators National Conference (MENC). (1990). *Data on music education.* Reston, VA: Author.

Rogers, G. L. (1982). Attitudes of high school band directors, band members, parents, and principals toward marching band contests. Unpublished doctoral dissertation, Indiana University.

Soundpost, 3(8) (Spring 1992), 9.

International Curriculum Developments

America has a long tradition of adopting artistic ideas from other countries. Until well into the twentieth century, artists and musicians seemed to believe that some study in Europe was a prerequisite for a successful career. Americans, however, were not so quick to adopt ideas about education from other countries. For 150 years, educators apparently felt America's great experiment in universal education had little to learn from the educational practices of other countries.

Music educators, on the other hand, have shown interest in four significant approaches or methods from other countries: those of the Swiss music educator Émile Jaques-Dalcroze, the Orff Schulwerk from Germany, the Kodály concept of music education from Hungary, and the Talent Education program of Suzuki in Japan. The reason for the interest of American music teachers in these four programs is not hard to pinpoint: Each has produced highly impressive results with its students that have attracted the attention of music teachers in the U.S. since the 1960s.

DALCROZE APPROACH:
DEVELOPMENT AND BACKGROUND

Émile Jaques-Dalcroze (1865–1950) began teaching music at the Geneva Conservatory in Switzerland shortly before the turn of the twentieth century. Music study at that time was divided into segmented courses such as harmony, sight-singing, form and analysis, and so on. Jaques-Dalcroze observed that many students seemed to know music only in an intellectual way.

He especially noticed that students who had trouble performing rhythmic patterns had no problem with rhythmic motor activities such as walking. From these observations he concluded that people instinctively have musical rhythm, but they do not transfer these instincts to music. He started experimenting with this idea by having students walk to music at different tempos. Slowly, more parts of the body were asked to respond to music. In this way, he developed an approach for learning music that had three main parts: (1) eurhythmics—rhythmic response to music; (2) solfège—singing with syllables; and (3) improvisation.

The idea of responding physically to music was revolutionary in Geneva in 1902. (The students in Jaques-Dalcroze's classes were barefooted and wore comfortable clothing!) He soon left the Conservatory, opened his own studio, and continued to experiment. Later, a group of Geneva businessmen set up a school for him in Hellerau, Germany. Between 1910 and 1914, interest in his method grew greatly. The outbreak of World War I in 1914 caused him to leave Germany and to establish the Institut Jaques-Dalcroze in Geneva, which is now part of the Conservatory of Music.

Although Jaques-Dalcroze thought his method could not be understood just by reading about it, he did write down some of his exercises. In *Rhythm, Music and Education*, he presents a list of twenty-two kinds of exercises for each of the three branches of his approach under the headings "Rhythmic Movement," "Solfège or Aural Training," and "Piano Improvisation." His approach, however, depends almost entirely on personal instruction.

The method—referred to as the "Dalcroze approach"—was introduced in the United States in about 1915. Public schools could not provide time or space for it to be taught in its authentic form, which was the only way Jaques-Dalcroze wanted it taught. Some teachers, however, adapted his ideas and, in other cases, teachers were influenced by the approach without being aware of it. By the 1930s, several college music schools or physical education departments were requiring courses in eurhythmics, the term often used for Dalcroze-like instruction. The interest in it leveled off at that point and then began to decline.

Characteristics of the Dalcroze Approach

1. A physical response to music is fundamental to the Dalcroze approach, and it somewhat dominates the early lessons. This aspect is the one for which it is best known. It is called "eurhythmics," meaning "good rhythmic flow" in Greek. The purpose of the movement is to create rhythmic sensitivity in the students by making them feel musical rhythm in their entire bodies. Musical concepts are also reinforced through physical movements.

The physical movements are not predetermined, but rather are the spontaneous products of each individual. Therefore, great differences are usually seen in the responses of a group of students to the same music.

The rhythmic example cited here from an adaptation of Jaques-Dalcroze's book is provided to give a clearer idea of the type of activity that takes place in the classes.

> *Exercise 1. Following the Music, Expressing Tempo and Tone Quality*
> The teacher at the piano improvises music to which the pupils march (usually in a circle) beating the time with their arms (3/4, 5/8, 12/8, etc.) as an orchestra leader conducts, and stepping with their feet the note values (that is, quarter notes are indicated by normal steps, eighth notes by running steps, half notes by a step and a bend of the leg, a dotted eighth and a sixteenth by a skip, etc.). The teacher varies the expression of the playing, now increasing or decreasing the intensity of tone, now playing more slowly or more quickly; and the pupils "follow the music" literally, reproducing in their movements the exact pattern and structure of her improvisation.

2. The second main branch of the Dalcroze approach is solfège, in which the familiar pitch syllables are used, but *do* is always C, *di* is C#, and so on. Jaques-Dalcroze thought that solfège singing developed the ability to listen to and remember tonal patterns. Singing and hand positions for designating the level of pitches of the scale are used in learning solfège, and these activities precede experience with notation.

Much emphasis is placed on inner hearing—the ability to imagine music in the mind. Students in Dalcroze classes sing intervals and songs with syllables. Some measures in the song are sung aloud, while others are sung silently in the mind.

3. Improvising, an integral part of eurhythmics and solfège activities, is the third main branch of the Dalcroze approach. Jaques-Dalcroze believed that each student should have the experience of expressing his or her own musical ideas.

Improvisation is begun on percussion instruments or with the voice. Sometimes a child is given one measure to which he or she improvises a response while maintaining the basic beat. Spoken commands or signals are given while improvisation is going on. This practice makes the students listen carefully and encourages skill development. For example, while executing a rhythmic pattern with their feet, they may be asked to do a contrasting pattern with their arms.

After the students have successfully improvised with their voices and on percussion instruments, they begin to improvise on the piano. Improvising at the piano is emphasized for advanced students and teachers.

ORFF SCHULWERK

Carl Orff (1895–1982) was a recognized twentieth-century composer. His best-known work is *Carmina Burana*. He started Schulwerk (the German word for "school work") in Munich in 1924 with Dorthea Günther. At that time, music education in Europe was heavily influenced by Jaques-Dalcroze, and there were numerous schools for gymnastics and dance. What made Schulwerk different was its primary focus on music. The school grew and in time had an ensemble of dancers and an orchestra, with the players and dancers being interchangeable. The group toured Europe and attracted much favorable attention.

During World War II, the school was destroyed and the instruments lost. Orff did not resume his educational activities until 1948 when he was asked by Bavarian radio to present a program of music for children. The request caused him to rethink his views on music education. The earlier school with Günther had been for teenagers. Orff began to realize the educational process should start much earlier with young children.

> I began to see things in the right perspective. "Elemental" was the password, applicable to music itself, to the instruments, to forms of speech and movement. What does it mean? The Latin word *elementarius*, from which it is derived, means "pertaining to the elements, primeval, basic." What, then, is elemental music? Never music alone, but music connected with movement, dance, and speech—not to be listened to, meaningful only in active participation. (Orff, 1990, p. 143)

The reborn Schulwerk was a success, and what started as a single broadcast was continued for five years. Five basic volumes of Schulwerk music were published between 1950 and 1954. Regular courses in Schulwerk were started in 1949 at the Mozarteum in Salzburg, Austria, under the direction of Gunild Keetman. The Orff Institute was established there in 1963. Although five books of Orff's music for children are available, he intended them to serve only as models for what children can do. In no sense do they constitute a course of study.

Schulwerk does not have a set course of study. "Those who look for a method or ready-made system are rather uncomfortable with Schulwerk," Orff said. The lack of an established set of procedures leads to different actions and results under the heading of Schulwerk. Orff himself said, "Unfortunately, it [Schulwerk] has often been misinterpreted, exploited, and falsified to the point of caricature."

Orff's interest in "elemental" music may seem a bit unusual. It derives from a theory about human development that believes children's musical development roughly corresponds to the development of music. According to this theory, rhythm preceded melody, and melody preceded harmony. It is not necessary to agree with this theory in order to teach aspects of Schulwerk.

Orff's ideas have been studied by many American music educators. By 1980, about two-thirds of the elementary music specialists in the United States participated in workshops on Schulwerk, with nearly a quarter of those teachers receiving four or more weeks of special training in it (Hoffer, 1981).

Orff's ideas are thriving today in the American Orff-Schulwerk Association (www.aosa.org). This association holds a national conference each year and sponsors summer workshops around the country that lead to certification in the Orff method. It also publishes a journal, *Echo*, that contains articles and reports of research related to the Orff method.

Characteristics of Schulwerk

1. Speech rhythms are an important part of the early instruction in Schulwerk. The children chant out rhymes, calls, and traditional sayings in a vigorous rhythmic fashion. For instance, short phrases for chanting can be derived from the pattern of the students' names (Kraus, 1990).

Mar-i-lyn   Mar-i-lyn   Ton - y   Mike

Meter and accent are also introduced in speech patterns. The students sometimes chant a phrase or sentence in canon—a spoken round. As the children become more adept at speech patterns, they are introduced through them to phrasing, dynamics, and styles such as legato and staccato. Simple forms such as rondo can also be introduced through speech patterns. These patterns are often combined with patterns of body rhythms: clapping; snapping the fingers; and patschen (thigh slaps), which are characteristic in Schulwerk. A pattern of clapping and thigh slapping can become a theme, for example, and it can be varied, repeated, performed antiphonally, or as the *A* part of a rondo.

2. Singing experiences follow the work done with speech patterns, which adheres to Orff's idea that melody follows rhythm. Singing at the early stages contains many short phrases sung back and forth between teacher and students and between the students in the group.

The first interval learned is *sol-mi*, the descending minor third. Unlike the Dalcroze method, however, the syllables are movable, not fixed. Intervals are introduced in a certain sequence. After *sol* and *mi* comes *la*, then *re*, and then *do*, which completes a pentatonic scale. Major and minor scales are taught later. Orff favored the pentatonic scale because he found it more natural. Also, half steps with their strong melodic tendencies are avoided when improvising.

3. Movement is an important part of Schulwerk as conceived by Orff, but it is not utilized as much in American adaptations of it. Orff's views about the value and purpose of bodily movement are similar to those of Jaques-Dalcroze. The natural untrained actions of children are the basis for movement. Running, skipping, hopping, and other physical movements are part of the students' musical development.

4. Improvisation is central to Schulwerk, and it is utilized in all of the activities—speech, movement, singing, and instrument playing. The initial efforts at improvising are highly structured. A child is given a limited number of pitches to use in creating a short melodic or rhythmic fragment of a specified length. Often these first efforts involve only *sol* and *mi* for one or two measures. As students gain experience in improvising, more pitches are added, and the patterns are made longer and more complex.

5. Instrument playing is an important aspect of Schulwerk. Not just any instrument is acceptable in the program, however. Orff wanted children's ears to become accustomed to the sounds of quality instruments. Furthermore, he wanted the instruments to be easy to play, and he favored those that had a "primitive appeal." So he had simple mallet instruments constructed that were capable of carrying the melody: xylophones, metallophones, and glockenspiels in various sizes.

After the original instruments were mostly destroyed in World War II, Orff worked with Klauss Becker, who developed the Studio 49 instruments found in many Orff classes today (see Figure 11.1). Not

Figure 11.1   Studio 49 Instruments

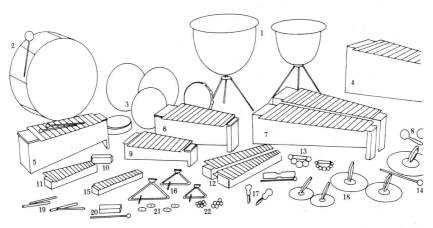

1 Kettle drums	9 Soprano xylophone	17 Castanets
2 Bass drum	10 Box rattle	18 Hanging cymbals
3 Tambours (hand drum)	11 Alto glockenspiel	19 Claves
4 Bass xylophone	12 Alto-soprano glockenspiel	20 Wood block
5 Alto metallophone	13 Bell spray	21 Finger cymbal
6 Alto xylophone	14 Felt head beater	22 Sleigh bells
7 Alto-soprano xylophone	15 Soprano glockenspiel	
8 Gourd	16 Triangles	

only do these instruments have a good tone quality and come in several sizes, they are useful in improvising because any unneeded bars can be removed temporarily so the student doesn't strike them accidentally. Schulwerk instruments are not considered toys, but rather an important means for making music. Most of the playing is done from memory or is improvised, which frees students from the need to read music.

6. Reading music comes only after several years of training. Even then, its main function is to preserve improvisations and arrangements.

7. Orff's music, and the music used and created in Schulwerk, have a strong folk-like character. It contains short, energetic melodic ideas; many ostinatos; simple harmonies; and an almost primitive quality at times.

KODÁLY APPROACH: DEVELOPMENT AND BACKGROUND

Like Orff, Zoltán Kodály (1882–1967; pronounced "Koh-**die**-ee") was a recognized twentieth-century composer. The folk opera *Háry János* is his best-known work, but he had many successful compositions. He was a friend and colleague of Béla Bartók, with whom he studied and collected Hungarian folk songs. Kodály was also greatly interested in the music education of children. "No one is too great to write for children," he wrote. "Quite the opposite—one should strive to be worthy of this task" (Kraus, 1990). Living up to his word, Kodály composed about twenty books of music for school students. They begin with very simple material for preschool children and continue through four-part works of great difficulty. In addition, he guided his native Hungary in the establishment of an exemplary program of music education in its schools.

World War II and the Nazi occupation of Hungary delayed the implementation of Kodály's educational ideas until after 1945. A new educational system was being established. In spite of the political limitations of being occupied by the Soviet Union, circumstances provided an unusual opportunity to design a new music program. Education in Hungary was controlled by the national government and had a heritage of strict academic training, which made it possible to institute a strong national program in this nation of ten million people.

Under Kodály, most children in the elementary schools of Hungary then received two periods of music each week. Through the fourth grade, music was taught by classroom teachers who had much more collegiate training in music than their American counterparts. From grades 5 through 8, music was taught by specialists.

The portion of Hungary's music education program that especially impressed foreign observers was its Music Primary Schools. These schools were similar to other elementary schools except for one important difference: The students received music instruction taught by a music specialist each day. Parents applied to these schools on behalf of their children, who were then selected on the basis of music tests (Carder, 1990).

The Music Primary School program began to attract international attention after presentations by Hungarian music educators and their students at conferences of the International Society of Music Education in 1958, 1961, and especially 1964, when Kodály himself addressed the conference. Since the mid-1960s, a number of American music educators traveled to Hungary to observe or study the program, and several Hungarian music teachers have taught workshops in the United States. By 1980, nearly half of the elementary music specialists in the United States had taken workshops in the Kodály approach, and over 12 percent received more than four weeks of training in it (Hoffer, 1981).

Kodály's method is alive and well in America. The Organization of American Kodály Educators (www.oake.org) has chapters in most states, holds a yearly national conference, and publishes a quarterly journal, *Kodály Envoy*. Unfortunately, the years following the end of Soviet Russian rule and the introduction of self-rule have not been good for the Kodály program. Today it is much weaker than it was in previous decades.

Characteristics of the Kodály Program

1. Kodály saw the purpose of music education as the creation of a musically literate population. "Is it imaginable that anybody who is unable to read words can acquire a literary culture or knowledge of any kind? Equally, no musical knowledge of any kind can be acquired without the reading of music" (Kodály, 1969).

Before developing the Music Primary School program, Kodály made an intensive study of the existing systems of teaching music in many countries. From England he adopted two techniques. One was a system of hand signs developed about a century earlier by an Englishman, John Curwen. The other, which is closely related to the hand signs, is their use in combination with pitch syllables. In movable *do,* the tonic note in major is always *do*. Therefore, the syllables represent relative pitch relationships, not fixed pitches as they do in solfège.

Figure 11.2   Curwen Kodály Hand Signs

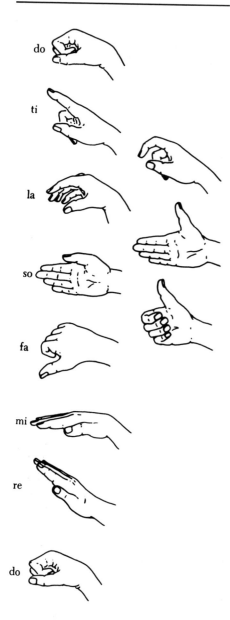

The hand positions, which are a form of kinesthetic reinforcement of the relative pitch, were altered slightly by Kodály from Curwen's hand signs (see Figure 11.2). Kodály also adopted Curwen's idea of abbreviating the syllable names to only the first letter. These letters are not intended to replace standard pitch names. Instead, their purpose is to aid in learning pitch relationships.

Pitch syllables are presented in an order similar to that used in Orff's Schulwerk: *sol, mi, la, do, re*, and then later in second or third grade *fa* and *ti*. In later years, *fi, si*, and *ta* are added, and music that modulates is sung with these syllables. During the primary years of instruction, much of the music sung is pentatonic. The pentatonic scale is strongly rooted in Hungarian folk music.

2. Learning patterns and motives are important aspects of the Kodály approach. For the most part, they are derived from music the students are singing. The more common patterns are practiced persistently. In this way, the students develop a sense of syntax for music.

3. Rhythm patterns are also taught by relating them

to the material being sung. Rhythmic values are initially represented by a vertical line or stem for a quarter note and by a pair of vertical lines joined together at the top by a brace or ligature for eighth notes, as in the example below. This type of notation is often referred to as "stick notation."

$$\frac{2}{4} \ | \ | \ | \ \sqcap \ | \ |$$

Figure 11.3   Pictorial Presentation of Notes and Their Lengths

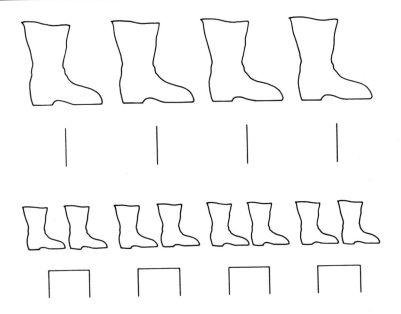

4. Music in the Kodály program is largely taught through singing. He was a strong believer in using the voice: "Only the human voice, which is a possession of everyone, and at the same time the most beautiful of all instruments, can serve as the basis for a general music culture" (Kraus, 1990). Recorder playing is introduced in second or third grade after a solid foundation has been built through singing.

5. One of the reasons Kodály so strongly favored unaccompanied singing was his wish to have children develop an accurate sense of pitch and the ability to hear music in their minds. Their intonation was impeccable and their vocal timbre very pure.

Many activities are designed to develop inner hearing. In addition to paying careful attention to intonation in both unison and part singing, the students sing music silently in their minds. A song is sung aloud until the teacher signals silence, at which time the students continue it in their minds. Singing aloud is resumed on another signal from the teacher.

6. Kodály was convinced that music instruction should start at an early age, well before children enter elementary school.

> Obviously, all reasonable pedagogy has to start from the first spontaneous utterances of the child, rhythmic-melodic expressions with repeated simple phrases which slowly give way to more complex structures. Since children learn most easily between the ages of three and six, the kindergartens would be able to accomplish much more in music if they would observe this pedagogic principle. (Kraus, 1990, p. 75)

7. The music used for the first several years of the curriculum consists largely of Hungarian folk songs. The association of the Kodály method with its folk and nationalistic roots is something that was often overlooked by foreigners. Hungary is a rather small nation with a population about the size of Ohio. Several times in its history it has experienced long occupations by outsiders—Turks, Austrians, Germans, and Russians. Two things made it possible for Hungarians to retain their national identity under such circumstances: their language (which is most closely related to Finnish) and their music. Therefore, knowledge of music is especially significant to Hungarians.

8. The Kodály program emphasizes music of a high quality. No commercial popular music is found in the program. "In art," he wrote, "bad taste is a real spiritual illness. It is the duty of the school to offer protection against this plague. . . . The goal is: To educate children in such a way that they find music indispensable to life . . . of course good artistic music" (Kraus, 1990).

SUZUKI TALENT EDUCATION: DEVELOPMENT AND BACKGROUND

With the work of Shinichi Suzuki (1898–1998), this chapter shifts from vocal-general music to instrumental music. Suzuki's views on teaching the violin are heavily laced with the belief that musical talent is a product of one's upbringing. "All human beings are born with great potentialities," Suzuki said, "and each individual has within himself the capacity for developing to a very high level" (Kendall, 1966, p. 9). The belief in the universal nature of music talent led to the inclusion of "Talent Education" in the name of the program.

Suzuki's father owned a violin factory, and he learned about violins and how to play them as a boy. His study also included eight years in Berlin in the 1920s. Before World War I he formed a string quartet with three brothers and also did some teaching. After World War II he started teaching young people. Many of his first students were orphans from the war.

His accomplishments as a teacher first became known in the United States in 1958 at a meeting of the American String Teachers Association at Oberlin College, when a film of 750 Japanese children playing Bach's *Concerto for Two Violins* was shown. A year later, John Kendall traveled to Japan to observe Suzuki at work. In 1964, the American String Teachers Association presented Suzuki and ten of his students, who ranged in age from ten to fourteen, at the NAfME national conference in Philadelphia. The impact on the audience was electrifying. Few of the teachers in the audience had ever heard young violin students play so musically. For several reasons that will become clear shortly, the impact of the Suzuki approach in the public schools has been somewhat limited, but his ideas have certainly been influential.

The work of Suzuki is very much alive in the United States today through the Suzuki Association of the Americas (visit their website at www.suzukiassociation.org). Its activities include a teacher development and certification program, summer workshops, and a quarterly publication, *American Suzuki Journal*.

Characteristics of Suzuki Talent Education

1. Suzuki strongly favored beginning instruction at an early age—in fact, the younger the better. Violin instruction in the Talent Education program usually begins at three years of age, but it can begin earlier. He favored playing good recordings for children while they are still in the crib. For several weeks before a child's first lesson, every day the parents should play the recordings of the pieces that will be studied later. Then the child attends a few lessons, watches and listens to what is going on, and is given an instrument.

String instruments, unlike most other instruments, can be adjusted in size, which facilitates working with young children. Many of Suzuki's youngest pupils begin on a 1/16th-sized violin. As they grow larger, they are given larger instruments until they play a full-sized violin.

2. The method of learning is rote imitation. The student hears something and attempts to imitate it. Suzuki believed that music is learned in much the same way that language is learned: "All children in the world show their splendid capacities by speaking and understanding their mother language, thus displaying the original power of the human mind" (Kendall, 1966, p. 9). The imitation of an aural model is an aspect of Suzuki's pedagogy that seems to be often overlooked. Not only does it help the students to play musically and without the mechanical qualities often associated with beginning instrument study, but it also appears to guide students through technical problems, sometimes even those for which they have had no specific instruction.

3. Everything the students perform is memorized. Technical matters of playing music on the instrument are learned first, and then students may begin looking at notation. Of course, reading by three-year-old children is out of the question, because their eye muscles have not developed sufficiently to allow them to focus on objects the size of music notation. The parents use the books and follow the music to help their children practice, however. When reading is introduced after some years of study, the process is one of following the notation of a work that the student already knows. In this way, the logic of music notation is more easily understood because it's a process of visualizing what has already been learned.

4. Whatever is learned by the students is learned thoroughly. While students are playing a work such as Vivaldi's *Concerto in A Minor*, the teacher may direct them to do knee bends or walk up and down stairs. Sometimes a group of students is divided in half. One half plays while the other half follows along silently, ready to pick up the music on a moment's notice without causing a break in the flow.

5. One of the parents, usually the mother, attends the lessons and learns the violin along with the child, at least at the beginning level. Suzuki wanted the parents involved in order to impress the child with the importance of the activity, and also to help in guiding practice at home.

6. Lessons are private and quite short, especially for the younger students. If a child yawns, the lesson is concluded. The students and teacher stand throughout the lesson. Often other children observe a lesson and perhaps join in playing a piece of music.

7. All students, regardless of ability, learn the same sequence of music. Some students may learn it faster than others, but all study the same works in the same order. Therefore, all Suzuki students have the same repertoire, which makes it easy to combine them for large group performances without prior rehearsals. There is almost a complete lack of etudes and scales, which are dear to the hearts of many instrumental music teachers. Instead, shifting, vibrato, bowing, and so on are dealt with in relation to their appearance in works of music. Technical exercises are drawn from passages in the music being studied. Suzuki avoids what he termed "manufactured material" before advanced levels are achieved.

8. The ten manuals or books contain carefully selected music, much of it by Bach, Handel, and Vivaldi. Recordings made by professional violinists are used.

9. Cooperation, not competition, is fostered among the students. Students of all levels of advancement play together and older students help the younger students.

Suzuki-like instruction is available from private teachers in many cities in the United States. Also, adaptations of Suzuki's ideas for teaching the violin have been made for viola, cello, bass, piano, flute, recorder, guitar, and harp. The only concession to size on the piano is the use of a box to make it easier for small children to reach the pedals. Clearly, America is not Japan, and a number of cultural factors make some of Suzuki's ideas difficult to carry out here. Nevertheless, many students who have started in Suzuki programs in this country have succeeded very well.

FOREIGN METHODS IN AMERICAN SCHOOLS

Music teachers who approach their work as professionals constantly examine and consider new teaching ideas. One source of fresh ideas is the successful methods developed in other countries. As successful as many of these methods are in their native land, American music educators should keep several facts in mind about adopting or adapting them.

It is not possible to pick up an educational program from Hungary or Japan or any other country (except maybe Canada) and drop it intact in the United States. Why? Because there are significant musical, educational, and cultural differences between each country and the United States. A musical difference, for example, can be found in the use of 6/8 meter. Many children's songs in America (e.g., "Pop Goes the Weasel" or "When Johnny Comes Marching Home") are in 6/8, but are not common in Hungary. In that country, the introduction of 6/8 meter is held off until the fourth grade, which would not be sensible in America. On the other hand, the pentatonic scale is found frequently in Hungarian folk music, but it is not common in American folk music.

There are also important educational differences among the countries of the world. Schools in most European countries have a shorter school day than American schools, but they do not offer extracurricular activities or provide lunches. The one or two hours that this makes available to European school students can be used in a variety of ways, one of which is music study at a community music school.

American music educators also need to keep in mind that Schulwerk and Suzuki violin instruction are almost never taught in the public schools of the countries with which they are associated. They were designed for and are taught in private schools that charge the students tuition. Dalcroze eurhythmics is taught in a few public school systems in Swiss cities, but seldom in the schools of other countries.

Cultural differences exist among nations, some of which are subtle. For example, while observing Suzuki's work in Japan, John Kendall talked with a sixteen-year-old boy who was studying violin. Although he planned to become an engineer, the young man was faithfully practicing the violin a couple of hours each day. The high school he attended did not have an orchestra for him to play in and community orchestras were rare in Japan. Kendall realized that the boy had no place to play the violin with others, and probably would not in the future. Why then, Kendall asked him, was he working so diligently at the violin? "Because it is good for my soul," the young man responded (J. Kendall, personal communication, April 1965). It is difficult to imagine a similar response from a sixteen-year-old American student.

Although it may be hard to transplant a music teaching approach that works well in Germany or Japan to the United States, it is quite easy to adopt some techniques from a method. Kodály himself adopted John Curwen's hand signs, which can easily be adopted by American music teachers. The same is true of some techniques from each of the methods described in this chapter. There is, however, more to each of these methods than their techniques. Jaques-Dalcroze, Orff, Kodály, and Suzuki gave music educators more than a few teaching recipes, gimmicks, or how-to-teach procedures. Just having students put on leotards and move to music does not mean one is teaching eurhythmics, any more than playing an ostinato or a metallophone means that one is following the Orff method. Although the methods contain the features listed in this chapter, there is much more to them than those features.

Questions

1. In what ways are the methods of Émile Jaques-Dalcroze and Carl Orff similar?
2. In what ways are the methods of Carl Orff and Zoltán Kodály different?
3. What are the differences between solfège (fixed *do*) and movable *do*?
4. Why does the Orff-Schulwerk program begin with speech patterns?
5. How do hand signs or other hand movements help students to sing on pitch more accurately?
6. Why did Kodály favor singing instead of playing instruments in the early grades?
7. In what way is the Suzuki method of learning to play the violin similar to the way children learn to speak?
8. Why is it necessary for American music teachers to adapt methods that were developed in other countries?

Project

Interview an elementary music specialist about the contributions of Dalcroze, Orff, or Kodály. Ask specifically about the benefits of the particular approach for American students and the points in the method that need to be adapted for use in American schools.

References

Becknell, A. F. (1970). A history of the development of Dalcroze eurhythmics in the United States and its influence on the public school music program. Doctoral dissertation, University of Michigan.

Carder, P. (Ed.). (1990). *The eclectic curriculum in American music education: Contributions of Dalcroze, Kodály, and Orff* (2nd ed.). Reston, VA: Music Educators National Conference.

Dobbs, J. (1968, August). Some great music educators: Émile Jaques-Dalcroze. *Music Teacher, 47*(8), 13.

Hoffer, C. R. (1981). How widely are Kodály and Orff approaches used? *Music Educators Journal, 67*(6), 46–47.

Huxley, T. H. (1968). On elemental instruction physiology. Quoted in J. Bartlett, *Bartlett's Familiar Quotations* (14th ed., p. 725). (E. M. Beck, Ed.). Boston: Little, Brown.

Kendall, J. (1966). *Talent education and Suzuki*. Reston, VA: Music Educators National Conference.

Kodály, Z. (1969). Visszatekintes (C. Russell-Smith, Trans.). In H. Szabo (Ed.), *The Kodály concept of music education.* London: Boosey and Hawkes. (Original work published 1964.)

Kraus, E. (1990). Zoltán Kodály's legacy to music education. In P. Carder (Ed.), *The eclectic curriculum in American music education: Contributions of Dalcroze, Kodály, and Orff* (2nd ed., pp. 79–92). Reston, VA: Music Educators National Conference.

Orff, C. (1990). The Schulwerk—its origins and aims (A. Walter, Trans.). In P. Carder (Ed.), *The eclectic curriculum in American music education: Contributions of Dalcroze, Kodály, and Orff* (2nd ed., pp. 137–144). Reston, VA: Music Educators National Conference.

Pennington, J. (1925). *The importance of being rhythmic: A study of the principles of Dalcroze eurhythmics applied to general education and to the arts of music, dancing, and acting.* Based on and adapted from *Rhythm, music and education* by É. Jaques-Dalcroze. New York: C. P. Putnam's Sons.

Challenges in Music Education

Charles Dickens begins *The Tale of Two Cities* with these memorable words: "It was the best of times; it was the worst of times." Although that sentiment is a bit strong when talking about the current condition of music education, it does contain an important thought for future music teachers to keep in mind. Yes, there are problems now, and there will be problems in the future. However, the opposite side of a problem is an opportunity, a chance to take corrective actions. It is through taking such actions that music education advances.

This chapter discusses a number of the problems/opportunities that music educators need to deal with now and in the near future. To the extent that they are successful in dealing with them, music education will continue to grow and improve. In a real sense, the future will largely be determined by those who teach music in schools today and in the future.

MUSIC IN EARLY CHILDHOOD

It is now estimated that nearly half of all four-year-olds receive some form of schooling. More than 76 percent of five-year-olds are in kindergarten (Digest of Education Statistics: 2014). These schools represent a major opportunity for music education.

Research evidence points to the importance of learning during children's early years. There are musical skills (matching pitch, for example) that they learn best when they are young; they don't learn

135

them as well later. Although teaching a child to sense the beat or sing a simple song may not appear to be a high-level musical or intellectual activity, it is extremely important in terms of a child's musical development. Not only is the particular musical skill involved, a child's attitude toward music is also affected. Children who don't do as well as their classmates in music usually realize it, which often gives them a negative attitude toward their participation in music and toward music in general. The approaches of Dalcroze, Orff, Kodály, and Suzuki discussed in the previous chapter emphasize the importance of teaching children music at an early age. Until recently, not enough American music educators believed that much more attention should be given to what children learn in music before first grade (*Soundpost*, 1992).

More and more school systems have begun to operate programs for children before kindergarten. State laws on education generally mention starting school at age five or six, but financial support for educating younger children is limited. The few existing regulations about education at this level usually cite physical plant specifications and adult/child ratios, but say little about curriculum. Most preschools are operated by churches, corporations, Head Start, or individuals. But quite a few public school districts are beginning to offer classes for four-year-old children.

Too often, the workers are not certified teachers. Many of them are hired at a low wage and have a limited education themselves. Preschools are often seen as providing children day care. In most instances, educational benefits seem to be a minor concern. The music the children usually receive, then, often consists of singing along with or engaging in physical actions to recordings. Some schools don't even do that.

Because so many preschool students are missing out on gaining musical skills, and because the learning of such skills is vital at an early age, NAfME formed a task force that developed a policy statement on music for preschool children and kindergartners. It reads, in part:

> Music is a natural and important part of young children's growth and development. Early interaction with music positively affects the quality of all children's lives. Successful experiences in music help all children bond emotionally and intellectually with others through creative expression in song, rhythmic movement, and listening experiences. Music in early childhood creates a foundation upon which future music learning is built. These experiences should be integrated within the daily routine and play of children. In this way, enduring attitudes regarding the joy of music making and sharing are developed. (*Soundpost*, p. 21)

To someone who plans to teach at the high school level, the music education of young children may not seem all that important. That is definitely not the case! Although the results of good music instruction may not show up for ten or more years, it will become evident sometime in improved musical skills and attitudes. The general level of musical interest and proficiency will have been raised.

MUSIC IN MIDDLE SCHOOLS

The problem of music for students in grades 6, 7, 8, and even 9 is a perennial one. Students in these grades are in a state of rapid transition from child to adult status. These grade levels contain a mixture of maturity and immaturity, which in itself is a challenge and opportunity.

Educators over the years have had a hard time deciding what type of education is best for students at this age. For many years, elementary schools went through grade 8; high school began with grade 9. There was no transition. Then came the junior high school, which was to be a junior version of high school, and included grades 7 through 9, with students moving from teacher to teacher for different subjects. Including ninth grade in this transition model, however, presented difficulties because ninth-grade courses had to meet certain criteria for inclusion on transcripts for college entrance.

The solution to these difficulties seemed to be the middle school, which was intended to be a real transition between elementary and high school. Middle schools, however, also present problems. Disagreement exists over the nature of the middle school curriculum. Some educators want middle schools to include exploratory experiences in certain areas, but not in basics such as mathematics and English.

In many middle schools music is included in the exploratory package—"the wheel"—of courses that are each six to nine weeks in length. The exploratory idea would be much more acceptable if there was room in the school day for it, say seven or even eight periods plus lunch. Unfortunately, many times the exploratory courses are jammed into a six-period day, which is the educational equivalent of trying to get a size 10 foot into a size 7 shoe.

Furthermore, music teachers don't agree on what music in the middle schools should be like. Sometimes the instruction, especially in performing groups, is very much like what is found in high schools. In other cases, general music classes are taught in a manner similar to what is provided to students in grades 4 and 5. The depressing fact is that many middle school students are not receiving much education in music education. One exploratory experience in grade 6 or 7 lasting for six or nine weeks can hardly be considered an adequate education in music.

The most worrisome point of all about inadequate middle school programs is that they are the culminating music instruction for many students. The majority of the students do not take music in high school, which means their music instruction concludes when they are eleven or twelve years old! Is it any wonder, then, that many Americans exhibit a twelve-year-old's understanding of music?

Assessment of Music Teaching

Finding out how well students in music classes learn what their teachers try to teach them has always been highly desirable. With the increased interest in assessment by school districts and state educational agencies, its importance has greatly increased. It represents a challenge for music teachers because they usually have had less time with students at the elementary school level. At the high school level the music program is dominated by performing ensembles, which have little tradition of assessing individual students' learning.

It is a fact: Music teachers already assess how their class or group performed a song or passage of music. This is fine—as far as it goes. It is limited, however, by the fact that it: (1) is not systematic, (2) evaluates the students only as a group, and (3) usually involves only a group's skill in performing music.

The evaluations of secondary school performing groups at contests and festivals consist of general comments and ratings on technique, intonation, and other musical aspects of an ensemble's performance of two or three prepared works. In many states the sight reading of one piece is also included. Some individual members of ensembles and pianists, usually the more able ones, also voluntarily enter solo competitions and receive comments and ratings on much the same basis as those given ensembles.

What else is needed for useful and well-balanced assessments?

1. *The learning of individual students needs to be assessed in an efficient way.* At first, assessment may seem like an enormously time-consuming task. It doesn't need to be, *if* the main purpose of assessment is to give teachers a more accurate idea of how well the students have learned. For example, it's not necessary to hear every member of a fifth-grade music class sing a song.

Instead, five or so students can be selected at random to sing a phrase of the song.

2. *The assessment process needs to be a conscious, systematic effort on the part of teachers.* They should know before a class or rehearsal what opportunities they might have to determine how much the students have learned. Furthermore, they need to keep a record of how well each student did. Keeping track of the hundreds of students a music specialist sees each week seems like a daunting task. It would be, *if* it involved a thorough assessment of every student. Instead, a simple three-part rubric (+, passable, –) is usually enough to provide a good idea of how well students have learned.

3. *More than performing skills needs to be assessed.* Students should gain information and understandings about music in addition to performing and creating it. They should be able to evaluate music and musical performances. An example of how this standard can be met could involve students who participate in a contest or festival. The teacher can have the students listen to several other groups and evaluate the performances of those groups using the same criteria that adjudicators use. The students can then bring their evaluations to the next rehearsal. An interesting and informative discussion could be held about aspects of performing music and how they are evaluated.

The attitudes that students acquire toward music are important, and they should not be left out of the assessment process. Teachers need to look for indicators of student interest such as songs requested, number of hands raised to answer questions, and even the expressions on the students' faces.

EDUCATION VERSUS ENTERTAINMENT

Music is fun. It's enjoyable. Those facts can be both a blessing and a curse. It is a blessing because people enjoy making and listening to music. It can be a curse when the entertainment value of music distracts students, teachers, and the community from the educational reasons for having music in the schools in the first place.

The education/entertainment dilemma affects very few areas of the school curriculum. No one thinks of learning about compounds in chemistry or practicing pronunciations in Spanish as entertaining.

The only other curricular area comparable to music in entertainment possibilities is physical education with its competitive sports.

The similarities between music and physical education are interesting, however. Both areas have general programs for all students. Both areas have specialists (coaches and directors) who are sometimes marginally involved with the general program. Both areas have performing groups (marching bands and competitive teams) that receive most of the attention but involve only a small percentage of the students.

There is another important way in which coaches of athletic teams and directors of performing ensembles are similar: They both present groups publicly, something that teachers in other areas almost never do. Public performance of music exerts pressure on teachers, some of which is actually self-imposed. In any case, the tendency for teachers is to do their best to present performances that impress audiences and adjudicators. Therefore, actions are sometimes taken to make the ensemble perform as well as possible. The teacher may decide to:

- Learn fewer works but perfect those works as much as possible
- Select music that will draw a positive response from the audience, which often means choosing more entertaining pieces
- Restrict membership to those students who are among the most capable
- Consider performance to be the main purpose of the ensemble

It takes a strong person to resist the temptation to slip over the line from teaching students to being producers of entertainment. As someone has pointed out, "The applause of an audience is a heady wine."

There are, however, several significant differences between athletic teams and music ensembles. Music groups earn grades and credits and meet during the school day because they are considered educational. The word "educational" is the key to the difference. The education of the athletic team members is limited to learning how to play the particular sport. In contrast, music ensembles should be the means by which students learn music.

As if pressures resulting from public performances weren't enough, music teachers teach an elective subject. They need to make their courses attractive so that enough students enroll to fill their teaching loads. In view of all these factors, it's not surprising that music teachers too often surrender to being producers of entertainment.

Part of the solution to handling the entertainment/education dilemma lies in reducing the pressures that music teachers think they need to use to appeal to audiences. Personal integrity is fine, but why make things more difficult than they need to be? Some of the pressure can be reduced by educating students, other teachers, school administrators and board members, and the community about the value and the purposes of music in the schools.

Part of this task must be assumed by each music teacher. NAfME and its state units can help raise the consciousness of people regarding the importance of music, and they can offer support. But in each school in each school district, it's the music teachers who must educate their principal and parents. Unless informed about the nature and the purposes of the school music program, very few administrators will know what that program should be and what it is trying to accomplish.

The importance of music for all students can be explained from two different viewpoints. One is through objective data about the importance of music throughout all civilizations and its importance in contemporary America. It is easy to assemble facts about the sums of money spent on recordings and concerts, the number of Americans who play instruments or sing in choral groups, and so on. These figures are impressive.

The other viewpoint involves subjective feelings. Most people sense—correctly—that music is a worthwhile activity. They feel good when they hear young people sing or play instruments, even if they can't express in words why they feel the way they do. These positive feelings are something that music education has going for it.

Maybe it's unfair that science and social science teachers don't have to educate people about the value of their subjects. Fair or not, it's a simple fact of life for music educators. It "comes with the territory," so to speak. Music teachers cannot afford to neglect this portion of their work.

FUND-RAISING

Fund-raising for school music groups is a two-edged sword. One edge is that fund-raising benefits many school music ensembles by helping them purchase needed material and equipment. In too many cases, the budget allocations for music are much too small to support an adequate program. In other cases, the extra funds allow for enrichment activities that can pump life into an ensemble program.

The negative edge of the sword is that fund-raising cuts deeply into the well-being of music in the schools. How? In four basic areas: (1) time and effort, (2) balance in the music program, (3) public image, and (4) the curricular status of music.

The first area, time and effort, is a concern because in many situations fund-raising consumes class or rehearsal time, and time is almost always in short supply for music instruction. In addition, extra effort is required on the part of both students and parents to raise funds. The music teachers involved must also commit their energies to such activities.

Fund-raising efforts are usually only for specific performing organizations, not the overall music program, which is the second way in which fund-raising is not helpful for school music programs. The groups for which funds are raised are given much visibility, while the other portions of the program (the ones involving the majority of the students) go largely unnoticed. Rarely does one hear about a fund-raising effort for fifth grade general music classes! The result is a major imbalance in many music programs. One or two performing groups become the music program in the eyes of most people, while the classes for most of the students are ignored.

In many communities, the group for which funds are raised is thought to be the measure of success for the entire music program. For example, the fact that one group raised money for a trip is seen as proof that the school district has a fine music program. Sometimes that assumption is accurate, but many times it is not. The quality of any one performing group in a school district often tells very little about the remainder of the program.

Fund-raising also carries with it baggage in terms of the image it presents, which is the third way the activity is not beneficial to music education. When most of the public's contact with school music is through fund-raising activities for trips to some attractive place, it's difficult for people to avoid forming a mental association between music and extracurricular activities. After all, students don't hold car washes or sell candy for history or math classes! Fund-raising encourages the view of music as a frill, something nice but not all that important. Fund-raising tends to undercut efforts to promote music as a worthwhile subject. When most of what people see of the school music program is its glitz and tinsel, it shouldn't be surprising when they fail to support it in times of limited budgets.

There is yet another way in which fund-raising can hurt school music programs. Once a music group establishes a record of success in securing funding, school administrators tend to let music take care of itself financially. The money saved on music, administrators logically conclude, can always be used for other needs in the school. Because of fund-raising activities, some directors of performing groups have virtually taken their music ensembles out of the school budget, whether they intended to do so or not.

NAfME developed a position paper on fund-raising. The full text of the policy appears in appendix C. The basic thoughts of the policy are simple. First, the curricular program of music instruction should be funded from the school budget. Second, there may be some enrichment activities for students in music classes that cannot normally be supported from the school budget. Third, fund-raising for these enrichment activities should be kept within reasonable limits, including avoiding the use of class or rehearsal time and large-scale projects that involve hundreds of hours and many thousands of dollars. Fourth, the success of the first three points in the policy statement depends on the willingness and ability of music teachers to provide guidance in fund-raising efforts. Fifth, fund-raising activities should not put youngsters at risk.

CULTURAL DIVERSITY

There are compelling reasons for music educators to teach various types of music in addition to traditional Western art and folk music. Every day the world is drawn more closely together. Television presents stories from every continent, and millions of people travel abroad each year. The world has become a global village. Furthermore, a continually growing number of students from a wide variety of nations and cultural backgrounds live in America and attend school. No longer is it likely that a young person can grow up having no exposure to at least a few persons from another country and culture.

The fact that there are good reasons for including a variety of types of music in school curricula does not mean it's easy to do well. Once again, there is the matter of time for instruction. If an elementary music specialist has only forty minutes a week with a class, adding more types of music presents a real challenge.

Second, no music teacher can teach all types of music well. Each type possesses subtleties that require training to understand and perform authentically. If music teachers have trouble knowing many different types of music, what about the students who don't know any kind of music well? This raises a dilemma: How far from the original character of a type of music can a performance stray before it becomes a travesty instead of a useful educational experience? There are no clear answers, of course, but it is a matter that music teachers should consider.

Third, music is very much intertwined with the culture in which it was created. This fact is both beneficial and detrimental. The good news is that music has a valuable role in helping students learn about the world's peoples. The negative side is that the close relationship with culture means the job of teaching many kinds of music is more difficult. It includes not only the musical sounds, but also the cultural and social setting of the music.

Fourth, the number of kinds of music around the world is huge. For example, one prominent ethnomusicologist estimated there are at least 500 different types of African music (Tracey, 1975). At best, a music teacher can cover only a tiny portion of the world of music.

Although it is not easy, music teachers should try to expand the types of music covered beyond what has been traditionally taught. These suggestions may help:

- Make a careful selection of music from the many different types found around the world, one that is as representative of the class's cultural backgrounds as possible.
- Spend enough class time on the selected works so they are really learned by the students. Skimming over many different pieces of music is not effective for most students.
- Present the music of non-Western cultures as authentically as possible. Usually this involves the use of videos, although sometimes a competent performer of a particular type of music lives in the community. Student performances can be attempted after the class has heard an authentic performance.
- Most important of all, try to instill in the students an attitude of respect and acceptance toward all kinds of music. The attitudes that students acquire about different kinds of music are much more important than what they learn in terms of information and skill in performing the music.

The need for a more diverse music curriculum presents music educators with an opportunity to develop music programs that are more varied and interesting. At the same time, in doing so they will be making their programs more representative of the pluralistic nature of American society.

STUDENTS AT RISK

Almost every social problem affects school students today—drugs, teenage pregnancies, broken families, morally questionable movies and television shows, and so on. In turn, these problems lead to a larger number of students coming to school who are unable or unwilling to learn and who will drop out before finishing high school. In America today, people who lack a high school education have real difficulties gaining employment at anything better than menial jobs.

Can music in the schools do anything to help students who are at risk, who are likely to drop out of school? Yes and no. The problems of most at-risk students are usually serious ones. Large and complex problems are not easily solved by any social or educational program, even ones that devote a lot of time and attention to the participants. Music instruction in the schools is simply not set up and supported in a way that provides anywhere near that degree or type of help. Therefore, the answer in many cases must be "no."

In some cases, however, the answer is "yes." Directors of high school performing groups often have the same students for a number of years. In addition, they see them not only in classes and rehearsals but also in informal situations, such as on tours. They often know their students better than any other teacher in the school. In fact, they sometimes know things about a student that even his or her parents don't know. For these reasons, music teachers can often influence students to a degree that other teachers cannot. Music teachers can easily become role models for their students.

The attraction of music groups for many at-risk students is something educators have sensed for many years, but it is rarely documented. When it is, the findings are impressive. One study uncovered that more than 70 percent of the secondary school principals interviewed could think of students who would have dropped out of school had it not been for the arts programs (Florida Department of Education, 1990). Such evidence, as well as casual observation, points to the fact that music can be a powerful force in helping at-risk students in school. Equally true, however, is the fact that music by itself is not a panacea for the social ills of young people and society.

The challenge for music educators is to attract more at-risk students into music programs than is presently the case. If most high schools offer only intensive and demanding performing groups, then the music program will touch a limited number of these students. Seldom can they afford the financial expense and personal commitment such groups demand. Therefore, music educators need to offer a wider variety of courses. A nonperformance course for the general students is a logical starting place for reaching more students. Other courses and music experiences should also be offered; e.g., ethnic music groups, keyboard, guitar, or a rock band. Fortunately, the 2014 standards include recommendations for these courses.

Many at-risk students are very active in and knowledgeable about popular music. The problem is not that they dislike music! Rather, the situation often seems to be that the school music program as it presently exists in so many secondary schools doesn't fit their musical interests and tastes. Should music teachers drop their successful band and choral groups to accommodate these students, or should they require that at-risk students shape up and learn the music being offered? Perhaps everyone should be more flexible and understanding than has often been true.

CLOSING THOUGHTS

Music educators can look back on a long and distinguished record of accomplishments by their profession. True, there are some storm clouds on the horizon (there always are) and challenges that need to be faced (also always true). And music education is not all that it should be. Perhaps one should look at music education like one might think about a dog walking on its hind legs. It's not that the animal walks imperfectly. Instead, it's amazing that the dog can do it at all. Music education has achieved much, often under difficult circumstances.

If you had been living in 1836 when Lowell Mason presented his proposal for music instruction in the Boston schools, and you had been asked to predict the prospects for the success of his idea, you probably would have said it was a nice but hopeless dream. To begin, music and the arts do not have the practical benefits that most other subjects can claim. Enriching the quality of people's lives does not have the same immediate, practical reasons for being a school subject. Few people have ever appeared to understand the true value of an education in music for all students. Furthermore, music has seldom enjoyed the financial and administrative support it deserves. It has had to struggle for time in the school day and for other forms of recognition.

Often music education seems to be caught in the middle regarding what it should be. On the one hand, it has to deal with what might be termed the "Joe Six-packs" view on the part of many school administrators and people in the community: Music is in the schools to provide entertainment, especially at athletic events. On the other hand, music education has to fend off the criticisms of those who consider themselves musically and/or intellectually superior, and who want an elite type of music education program that would reach only a small percentage of students.

Fortunately, music education defied what logically should have been the fate of a quiet burial. It has achieved a scope and size that would astound Lowell Mason were he, by some warp of time, to return and observe school music programs today. As long as music educators retain Mason's vision and passion for music for all students, there is no reason why music education cannot continue to grow and improve in the future.

QUESTIONS

1. Why is the music instruction of three- to six-year-old children so important?

2. Why is the limited music education that a majority of the students in middle schools receive a major weakness in American schools?

3. What special challenges does the accurate assessment of learning in music present to music educators?

4. Music is enjoyable and can often be entertaining. In what ways is this fact helpful to music education? In what ways is this fact detrimental to music education?

5. In what ways can fund-raising help a particular performing group?

6. In what ways can fund-raising hurt a school's music program?

7. Teaching various types of music in addition to traditional Western classical and folk music is very desirable. What are some factors that challenge music educators in doing this?

8. Why are music teachers often more effective in helping at-risk students than other teachers?

PROJECT

Think of a musical work that might be performed publicly by a school group. Answer the following questions about how that work could be used to educate an audience about music and music education. What aspects of that work should the audience be informed about? What aspects of what the students have learned from performing that work could be demonstrated for the audience?

REFERENCES

Digest of Education Statistics: 2014. U.S. Department of Education, National Center for Education Statistics, tables 41 and 43.

Florida Department of Education. (1990). *The role of fine and performing art in high school dropout prevention.* Tallahassee, FL: Author.

Music Educators National Conference (MENC). (1994). *Opportunity-to-learn standards for music instruction: Grades pre-K–12.* Reston, VA: Author.

Soundpost, 8(3) (Spring 1992), 21.

Tracey, Hugh. (1975). Personal communication.

Music Education
and *Mr. Holland's Opus*

Music teachers have almost never been featured in a motion picture. *Mr. Holland's Opus* is a genuine exception; even its title is different. The film's producers realized that the word "opus" is not an everyday word. What to do? They decided to keep the title and forgo the usual promotional efforts and ads. Instead, they decided to show the film at meetings of people who are interested in education and the arts. The producers believed, correctly as it turned out, that people who saw it would spread the word about it being a really good movie. More than half a million people were shown the film prior to its release. That represented a huge potential loss in future revenue from its regular admissions.

Fortunately, their confidence in the movie more than made up for the lost revenue. *Mr. Holland's Opus* was a major financial success. It cost an estimated $31 million to make, and in just its first year grossed over $106 million! It was also an artistic success. Actor Richard Dreyfuss was nominated for the Academy Award for Best Actor and the film was nominated for several other honors, including the Golden Globe Award for Best Screenplay.

THREE USEFUL QUESTIONS

If you have not seen this movie in a long time, you should watch it again (check your local library or download it from a streaming service). After you have done that, complete these three short projects:

1. Compare how Mr. Holland's views on teaching matured over the thirty years he taught at Kennedy High School. Recall his response to the principal's (Mrs. Jacobs) observation about his speed in getting to the parking lot at the end of the school day during his first year there. Compare it with his feelings about teaching with those he expressed to Coach Meister just before the event honoring him.

2. According to former clarinet player student and now governor Gertrude Lang, what was Mr. Holland's opus? Was it his first symphony, which had its premiere at the event in his honor, or was it something else?

3. In what ways did Glen Holland demonstrate that he really cared that each of his students learned? Think of his work with Gertrude Lang (clarinet player), Louis Rusk (drummer and wrestler), and Rowena Morgan (excellent singer). Were his efforts as great with the less talented students as they were with the talented ones?

FINAL ASSIGNMENT

This course has introduced you to the music education profession. What are your thoughts about being a school music teacher now? In less than twenty-five words, describe how you hope to be earning a living twenty years from now. Your answer will *not* affect your grade in this course!

Appendix A
The Music Code of Ethics

Music educators and professional musicians alike are committed to the importance of music as an essential component in the social and cultural fiber of our country. Many of the ways that they serve this commitment overlap—many professional musicians are music educators, and many music educators are, or have been, actively engaged in the field of professional performance. Based on training and expertise, however, educators and professional musicians serve fundamentally different functions:

- Music educators contribute to music in our society by promoting teaching music in schools, colleges and universities, and by promoting a greater interest in music and the study of music.

- Professional musicians contribute through their performance of music to the public in promoting the enjoyment and understanding of music. This Code is principally concerned with this role, though professional musicians also contribute by providing music for weddings, funerals, and religious ceremonies.

When the line between these different functions is blurred, problems may arise: Music educators may find that school programs they have built over the years are thrown into disarray. Musicians may suffer harm to their prestige and economic status. And those served by both educators and musicians—students and the public—may find that they are poorly educated and poorly entertained.

This Code of Ethics sets out guidelines that will help educators and performers avoid problems stemming from a lack of understanding of each others' role. It does not address the many other issues that shape ethical behavior in performance and in education.

Music educators and the student groups they direct should be focused on the teaching and learning of music and on performances of music directly connected with the demonstration of performances at:

- School functions initiated by the schools as a part of a school program, whether in a school building or other site
- Community functions organized in the interest of the schools strictly for educational purposes, such as those that might be originated by the parent and teachers association
- School exhibits prepared as a courtesy on the part of a school district for educational organizations or educational conventional organizations or educational conventions being entertained in the district
- Educational broadcasts that have the purpose of demonstrating or illustrating pupils' achievements in music study or that represent the culmination of a period of study and rehearsal. Included in this category are local, state, regional, and national school music festivals and competitions held under the auspices of schools, colleges, universities, and/or educational organizations on a nonprofit basis and broadcast to acquaint the public with the results of music instruction in the schools.
- Student or amateur recordings for study purposes made in the classroom or in connection with contest, festival, or conference performances by students. These recordings are routinely licensed for distribution to students, but should not be offered for general sale to the public through commercial outlets in any way that interferes with the normal employment of professional musicians.

In addition, it is appropriate for educators and the school groups they direct to take part in performances that go beyond typical school activities, but they should only do so where they have established that their participation will not interfere with the rights of professional musicians and where that participation occurs only after discussion with local musicians (through the local AFM). Events in this category may include:

- Civic occasions of local, state, or national patriotic interest, of sufficient breadth to enlist the sympathies and cooperation of all persons, such as those held by the American Legion and Veterans of Foreign Wars in connection with Memorial Day services

- Benefit performances for local charities, such as the Red Cross and hospitals (when and where local professional musicians would likewise donate their services)

Professional Musicians provide entertainment. They should be the exclusive presenters of music for:

- Civic parades (where professional marching bands exist), ceremonies, expositions, community-center activities; regattas; nonscholastic contests, festivals, athletic games, activities, or celebrations, and the like; and national, state, and county fairs
- Functions for the furtherance, directly or indirectly, of any public or private enterprise. This might include receptions or public events sponsored by chambers of commerce, boards of trade, and commercial clubs or associations.
- Any occasion that is partisan or sectarian in character or purpose. These occasions might include political rallies, private parties, and other similar functions.
- Functions of clubs, societies, and civic or fraternal organizations

Interpreting the Code is simple. This is not to say that the principles set forth in this Code will never be subject to differing interpretations. But if educators and performers keep to the core ethical idea, that education and entertainment have separate goals, conflict should be kept to a minimum. Additional considerations:

- School groups should not be called on to provide entertainment at any time—they should be involved exclusively in education and the demonstration of education. Statements that funds are not available for the employment of professional musicians; that if the talents of school musical organizations are not available, other musicians cannot or will not be employed; or that the student musicians are to play without remuneration of any kind, are all immaterial.
- Enrichment of school programs by presentations from professional entertainers does not replace a balanced, sequential education in music provided by qualified teachers. Enrichment activities must always be planned in coordination with music educators and carried out in a way that helps, rather than hinders, the job of bringing students the skills and knowledge they need. The mere fact that it may be easier for a school administration to bring in a unit from a local performing arts organization than to support a serious, ongoing curriculum in the schools has no bearing on the ethics of a professional entertainer's involvement.

Should conflicts occur in issues touched by this Code, the American Federation of Musicians (AFM) and NafME: The National Association for Music Education suggest that those involved:

- First, attempt to resolve the situation by contacting directly the other party involved.

- Second, attempt resolution through the local representatives of the associations involved. The local of the AFM is accessible through directory assistance. The officers of NafME state affiliates can be found through the NafME website (www.nafme.org) or by calling NafME headquarters at 1-800-336-3768.

- Finally, especially difficult problems should be resolved through mediation. Help with this mediation is available by contacting the national offices of the AFM and NafME.

This code is a continuing agreement that will be reviewed regularly to make it responsive to changing conditions. It is endorsed by the American Association of School Administrators, National Association of Elementary School Principals, National Association of Secondary School Principals, and International Association of Jazz Educators.

Appendix B
Music with a Sacred Text

The following is an abridgement of The National Association for Music Education's position on music with sacred texts.

Does music with a sacred text have a place in the public schools?

It is the position of NafME that the study and performance of religious music within an educational context is a vital and appropriate part of a comprehensive music education. The omission of sacred music from the school curriculum would result in an incomplete educational experience.

The First Amendment does not forbid all mention of religion in the public schools; it prohibits the advancement or inhibition of religion by the state. A second clause in the First Amendment prohibits the infringement of religious beliefs. The public schools are not required to delete from the curriculum all materials that may offend any religious sensitivity. For instance, the study of art history would be incomplete without reference to the Sistine Chapel, and the study of architecture requires an examination of Renaissance cathedrals. Likewise, a comprehensive study of music includes an obligation to become familiar with choral music set to religious texts.

The chorales of J. S. Bach, the "Hallelujah Chorus" from George Frideric Handel's *Messiah*, spirituals, and Ernest Bloch's *Sacred Service* all have an important place in the development of a student's musical understanding and knowledge.

In order to ensure that any music class or program is conforming to the constitutional standards of religious neutrality necessary in pub-

lic schools, the following questions raised in 1971 by Chief Justice War-
ren E. Burger in *Lemon v. Kurtzman* should be asked of each school-
sanctioned observance, program, or institutional activity involving religious content, ceremony, or celebration:

1. What is the purpose of the activity? Is the purpose secular in
   nature, i.e., studying music of a particular composer's style or
   historical period?
2. What is the primary effect of the activity? Is it the celebration of
   religion? Does the activity either enhance or inhibit religion?
   Does it invite confusion of thought or family objections?
3. Does the activity involve excessive entanglement with a religion
   or religious group, or between the schools and religious organizations? Financial support can, in certain cases, be considered
   an entanglement.

If the music educator's use of sacred music can withstand the test of
these questions, it is probably not in violation of the First Amendment.
   Since music with a sacred text or of a religious origin (particularly
choral music) constitutes such a substantial portion of music literature and has such an important place in the history of music, it should
and does have an important place in music education.

Religiously Neutral Programs

   With this volatile topic, music educators should exercise caution
and good judgment in selecting sacred music for study and program-
ming for public performances. During the planning phase of each program, the following questions should assist the teacher in determining
if the program is, indeed, religiously neutral:

1. Is the music selected on the basis of its musical an educational
   value rather than its religious context?
2. Does the teaching of music with sacred text focus on musical
   and artistic considerations?
3. Are the traditions of different people shared and respected?
4. Is the role of sacred music one of neutrality, neither promoting
   nor inhibiting religious views?
5. Are all local and school policies regarding religious holidays
   and the use of sacred music observed?
6. Is the use of sacred music and religious symbols or scenery
   avoided? Is performance in devotional settings avoided?
7. Is there sensitivity to the various religious beliefs represented
   by the students and parents?

Appendix C
Fund-Raising

NaFME regards music education as an integral part of the core curriculum in K–12 schools. In 2001 the federal government reauthorized the Elementary and Secondary Education Act, commonly known as the "No Child Left Behind" Act. The arts were included as one of the "core academic subjects." Therefore, financial support for music education must be part of the school's and district's regular curricular budget. When funds from these sources are not sufficient to maintain the quality program expected within that community, fund-raising may be required. The purpose for which the funds are raised should be clearly defined and purposefully directed toward enriching the music education of students. Funds raised through fund-raising activities should be strictly differentiated from local or district funds. In evaluating fund-raising activities, music educators should consider the overall effort to be expended, the financial return on that effort, and the demands fund-raising may make on their instructional time.

Concerns

School music groups' fund-raising efforts, especially at the high school level, seem to grow each year. Fund-raising can demand inordinate amounts of time and effort from music teachers, their students and the students' parents. Sometimes valuable instruction time is lost. If fund-raising activities benefit only one segment of the school music program, then other facets of that school's music program may suffer or be ignored. If not managed carefully, fund-raising activities may result in a loss of regular curricular budget funds and cause music to be classified as an "extracurricular activity" and therefore not eligible for school budget support.

If the music educator has a group of parents that periodically or regularly collect money or raise funds, the group should be officially recognized and endorsed by the school's administration. Also, the booster organization should be incorporated under that state's not-for-profit laws.

The Music Educator's Role

In any fund-raising activity, the music educator should be the project manager who is to:

- be knowledgeable about Board of Education and school policies regarding fund-raising and the fiscal and political ramifications of the effort. Note: Schools and districts differ regarding requirements and policies governing how money raised by booster organizations is to be handled, accounted for, and deposited. This is a critical facet of fund-raising that must be understood and adhered to by the music educator and the parents before any fund-raising activity is begun.

- coordinate fund-raising activities with other groups within the school that do fund-raising relative to timing of fund-raising activities and products or services being sold

- develop an overall plan in cooperation with school administrators, parents, and students for selecting an appropriate fund-raising activity; implementing the project; and tracking the money raised

- delegate the responsibility for record keeping, product handling, collection of funds, and accounting in accordance with school and district policies

Guidelines

Fund-raising should not supplant or replace regular school or district funding. Fund-raising may enrich music instruction by enabling activities and materials not normally funded from school or district budgets. It may also help music programs secure additional equipment and materials needed to enhance the curriculum. Students may benefit from supplementary educational experiences and educational field trips that meet NafME and the National Association of Secondary School Principals guidelines made possible by these funds. Fund-raising for these purposes is justifiable if kept within reasonable limits.

Fund-raising undertaken to enrich students' music education should:

- require minimal time and effort from students and teachers;
- use very limited or no instructional time;

- be appropriate for students; and
- adhere to the Code of Ethics of NafME, the American Federation of Musicians, the American Association of School Administrators, the National Association of Elementary School Principals, and the National Association of Secondary School Principals.

In addition, it is important that the ethical and legal implications of any fund-raising project be thoroughly understood in order to prevent jeopardizing the music teacher or the program, and to avoid situations that might result in litigation due to an accident or other misfortune. All fund-raising efforts should adhere to responsible standards of safety and well-being for the students involved.

Index